Simplified Furniture Design and Construction

Also by the Author

The New Archery
Winchester '73 and '76

Simplified
Furniture Design
and Construction

David F. Butler

South Brunswick and New York: A. S. Barnes and Company
London: Thomas Yoseloff Ltd

A. S. Barnes and Co., Inc.
Cranbury, New Jersey 08512

Thomas Yoseloff Ltd
108 New Bond Street
London W1Y OQX, England

SBN: 498 07345 9

Printed in the United States of America

My wife, *Ann Woodbridge Butler,* has long had an interest in early American furniture, and has worked with me on creating and building many of the projects described in this book.

It is to her that this effort is dedicated.

Contents

Preface

Like many young couples starting out on a small budget, my wife and I needed furniture, and did not have funds to purchase everything. We both had an interest in early American furniture, and put this interest to work creating the designs described in this book. If one does not have funds to buy furniture, then funds are not available to buy elaborate woodworking machinery and tools. The designs described in this book were created to utilize simple construction techniques and a minimum of tools and machinery. The projects have stood the test of time, and some are now over fifteen years old and still in excellent condition.

Many friends have helped with this book in discussions of designs and assembly techniques during the past twenty years. Special thanks are due to Mrs. Geraldine. A. Patti, for typing and retyping the manuscript in addition to her regular secretarial duties. Thanks are also expressed to Mr. John E. Woodbridge, who reviewed the manuscript carefully, and suggested many improvements.

Simplified Furniture Design and Construction

1

Tools and Workbench

Many people enjoy woodworking as a hobby. The excellent woodworking courses offered in high schools train several hundred thousand young men each year in the proper use of hand tools. Several million American homes have small shops in the basement where boys and girls learn woodworking skills from their parents. Others take up the hobby as a means for relaxation later on in life. If woodworking can be used to create objects which are truly useful, the hobby becomes doubly rewarding.

Many young couples find it an area where both can bring their own particular skills to bear. The husband may design and build the furniture while the wife applies her efforts to the finer operations of finishing the furniture. The finishing operations require knowledge of stains and fillers and the relative merits of such materials as shellacs, varnishes, and the newer synthetic finishes. Proper finishing provides a durable, rugged surface and in the process enhances the natural appearance of the wood.

The major problem that most woodworkers face is the need for elaborate machinery which is far beyond the financial reach of the average budget. The techniques of simplified construction described in this book allow the assembly of high quality, durable furniture with a minimum investment in tools. Half of the projects described in this book were built with no power tools at all, including the "Hutch" described in Chapter 9. Excellent furniture can be constructed this way but more time and effort are required than if better equipment is available.

It is essential to have a small set of high-quality woodworking tools in order to do worthwhile work. It is desirable to have a large, sturdy workbench which can be the focal point for your woodworking activities.

ESSENTIAL HAND TOOLS

The hand tools required for woodworking are few in number, but each should be of the highest quality. There is nothing more frustrating than to have long and patient work ruined because a dull chisel splits out a section of wood or a cheap hammer glances off a fastener and places a deep gouge in a polished wood surface. The following tools may be considered essential for furniture construction:

1. A good claw hammer.
2. Crosscut saw.
3. Ripsaw.
4. Standard hacksaw.
5. A good woodworking plane with a bottom surface at least 10 inches long.
6. A coping saw with a half dozen woodworking blades.
7. A woodworking square which will allow accurate layout of 90° and 45° angles.
8. A rubber mallet for tapping wood parts into place without damaging them.
9. A bit brace with screwdriver attachment which will save you a great deal of effort in driving a large number of screws.
10. Several screwdrivers.
11. A good ¼-inch chisel.

12. A good ⅜-inch chisel.
13. A good ½-inch chisel.
14. An oilstone to keep the chisels very sharp.
15. Coarse, medium, and fine files with crosscut patterns. A crosscut file is much better than a mill file for removing wood. At first, half-round files can be purchased, because these allow filing of either flat or rounded surfaces. Later, it is worthwhile to build up an inventory of flat, half-round, and full-round files of various sizes and patterns. Experience in your early woodworking projects will quickly show which additional sizes and patterns of files will be most useful for your type of work.
16. A coarse and a medium half round rasp.
17. Needle-nose pliers.
18. Standard pliers.
19. Lock-grip or vise-grip pliers with flat jaws. Vise-grip pliers provide an excellent way for clamping things together temporarily. They are also extremely useful for removing stubborn fasteners which have become jammed in place.
20. C clamps of several different sizes. C clamps with jaw openings of 3 inches and 5 inches have proved particularly useful.
21. Woodworking clamps are used to hold wide boards during the edge glueing process, and furniture during assembly. Clamps are available at some large lumber yards and at woodworking specialty houses which consist of a movable head and a sliding lower jaw. These are assembled to a piece of pipe which provides the required stiffness.
22. In addition to the hand tools, one portable power tool is very important—a ¼-inch electric drill. A good drill may be purchased for as little as $15, and you will use it more than any other single tool, particularly when it comes time to assemble the furniture.

A sanding disk may be purchased to go on the ¼-inch drill, but *never* use this sanding disk on exposed top or side surfaces of your furniture. It will leave circular marks on the wood that are very difficult to remove. The sanding disk is useful in hidden areas, and to remove wood from the end grain of boards, where a plane will not cut properly.

23. Two sets of drills. A graduated set of metal drills from 1/16 inch to ¼ inch in diameter and a second set of woodworking drills with reduced shanks to fit the ¼-inch chuck. These woodworking drills should cover the range from 5/16 inch through ½ or ¾ inch in diameter.

ADDITIONAL EQUIPMENT USEFUL IN WOODWORKING

As you become more interested in woodworking, some additional tools may be useful. These can include a small hand drill to work in tight places, countersinking bits to sink screw heads below the surface of the wood, and different patterns of files, chisels, and saws for your particular interest.

Two power tools are valuable time savers if you can afford them.

1. *Eight-inch circular saw.* The most valuable stationary power tool by far is the 8-inch circular saw with a tilting arbor. The saw should be equipped with an extension table on one side to give a broad working surface and a ½-horsepower electric motor. The flexibility of such a saw in woodworking is extremely broad. After the exact sizes of parts have been laid out on wood planks, the circular saw can rapidly cut the pieces to size. I usually make crosscuts with a handsaw, and the long cuts along the grain of the wood on the circular saw. If a fine-toothed blade is used, the cuts will be smooth and require only a light planing with the hand plane, and sanding.

The circular-saw blade may be removed and replaced by a carbide sanding disk. The carbide sanding disks come with a rough carbide grit on one side and a fine carbide grit on the other. This may be used to sand wooden surfaces. The circular sander does leave curved marks in the wood across the grain and these must be removed by the hand plane, or by hand sanding afterward. The rough side of the sanding disk may be used to shape wooden parts—acting much like a gigantic file. It is particularly useful for beveling surfaces and rounding edges where this kind of shaping is desirable.

With a tilt-arbor saw, the table always remains level. The saw blade may be angled to the table to make angular cuts. The angles may be adjusted by cutting scraps of wood until the exact relationships are established. Then when the angle cuts are put into good wood the joints will have the proper angular relationship to each other.

The circular saw may also be used as a grinding machine. A 5-inch medium grinding wheel may be placed on the arbor and used for rough grinding all types of tools, and shaping metal parts. A fine grinding wheel should be used for sharpening drills, chisels, and planes. Keep a can of water nearby and dip the tool edge into the water frequently. The cutting edge of a plane, drill, or chisel heats up very rapidly during grinding. If the edge starts to turn blue you have overheated the blade and made the steel soft. The discolored metal must be ground away before you will have a "tempered" hard steel cutting edge again. After grinding, the edges of these tool blades should be finished by honing on an oilstone. Place a small puddle of oil on the stone, and hone the edge of the blade with a circular motion.

Additional attachments such as molding heads with different-shaped cutters and groovers and dado cutters may be added to the circular saw to provide special curved moldings. These moldings can add a decorative touch to tabletops, legs, and shelves. These special cutters are also useful for cutting grooves in sideboards of bookcases to inset shelves.

2. *Power Jig Saw.* A second valuable power tool is a jig

saw, preferably with at least an 18-inch distance from the blade to the throat of the frame. The jig saw will not receive so frequent use as the circular saw, but it is a great time saver in cutting fancy shapes on decorative panels, and for fine cuts, such as the angles on frames. Special blades for cutting soft metal are available, in addition to the wood-cutting blades for a jig saw. These metal-cutting blades are very useful in cutting out brass or copper decorations, such as those shown on the "Bedside Table" in Chapter Two.

In cutting wood on the jig saw, it is best to use a wide blade for straight cuts and narrower blades where sharp curves are required.

Universal motor mounts are available so that the same electric motor may be used on both the jig saw and table saw, thus saving quite a bit of money. A motor of at least $\frac{1}{2}$ horsepower should be chosen to provide sufficient power for the circular saw.

Power tools are not necessary for good woodworking. Fully half the projects described in this book were done with no power tools other than a $\frac{1}{4}$-inch electric drill. Many lumberyards will cut wood to accurate dimensions for a very nominal extra charge when you purchase it. If your design is accurately laid out on paper, you may be able to take advantage of this service. Even if the lumberyard service is not available, the lumber for an average piece of furniture can be cut with hand saws in a relatively short period of time. No matter how the wood is finally cut, it is essential that the design be laid out to very accurate dimensions before the wood is sliced up into pieces.

THE WORKBENCH

If ample space is available, the very first woodworking project should be the construction of an adequate workbench. The bench described in this chapter has provided excellent service over a 15-year period. It has been installed in three separate locations, and is still strong and useful. (See FIGURE 1.) A large and sturdy vise is installed at one end of the bench. It is well

Figure 1

to stretch the budget and purchase the largest possible vise that you can afford. After I ruined several vises with a 3-inch opening, I finally secured a large rugged vise with a 5-inch opening which has proved tough enough to absorb all of the punishment that comes its way. A lightweight vise will spring as you try to bend and hammer parts and it will be a source of considerable frustration. A large vise installed close to the vertical leg of the bench at the left-hand end provides great rigidity when required. The workbench top is constructed of a single 4 x 8-foot sheet of ⅝-inch-thick plywood, which has been cut 30 inches from one side. In this way, the front half of the workbench is two-plies thick or a full 1¼ inches thick, while the rear half has only one thickness of plywood. The top is designed to be 37½ inches above the floor, which is a good working height.

One of the most difficult problems with a workbench is to design one which will not move while you are working on it. This bench takes advantage of the fact that almost all American homes are designed with a 16-inch spacing to the floor beams. The workbench is constructed with four 2 x 4-inch vertical beams at the back surface which run from the floor to the overhead beams of the ceiling above, and are bolted to the overhead beams. There are four horizontal supports under the workbench and four angle beams which run back from the horizontal support and tie into the vertical beams at floor level. There are two additional legs for extra support and these are set well back from the work surface.

The construction details of the workbench are shown in FIGURE 2. Three-eighths inch or ½-inch bolts are a good size to use for the construction. The result is a workbench which is very strong and sturdy in construction and yet has a lot of knee room underneath. All the supports are set back from the front surface or angled back so that you are not contantly running into things as you work. A 16-inch-wide shelf has been installed underneath the workbench by placing ¾-inch boards on the horizontal supports which are fastened to the two vertical legs. This horizontal shelf is extremely useful for holding heavy boxed tools such as sets of socket wrenches or electric drills and other heavy objects. Underneath the workbench on the right-hand side, two small drawers have been installed each of which contains sixteen compartments. These small drawers are handy to hold the most commonly used sizes of screws and nails. A few of each size are kept in the compartment for ready reference while construction of furniture is underway.

The hand tools are all hung on the backboard of the workbench. The backboard is a full 8 feet wide and extends from the top of the workbench to the ceiling of the room. It is constructed of 12-inch wide tongue-and-groove ¾-inch wood with

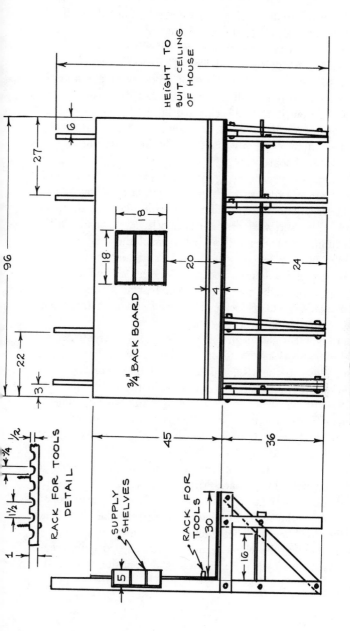

WORKBENCH

FIGURE 2

an 18 x 18-inch cutout in the center of the backboard to take a set of shelves. Along the lower surface of the backboard a wooden strip is installed with a series of cutouts which hold pliers, chisels, screwdrivers, and files. The easiest way to make this up is to cut 2-foot-long strips of wood with a scalloped shape as shown in the small detail of FIGURE 2. Make up one section, and screw it to the backboard at the left-hand end of the workbench. As that section becomes filled with hand tools, add another piece until you have finally filled up the entire length of the backboard.

In any kind of woodworking, it is essential that you know where tools are in order to work efficiently. An easy way to organize your small tools is to concentrate the pliers at the left-hand end, then screwdrivers, then chisels, and finally files. Since the number of files will probably equal the total number of the three other categories of tools, this arrangement means that all of the pliers, chisels and screwdrivers are within easy reaching distance of the vise. It is a good principle of modern industrial management to locate the most frequently used tools closest to your normal working position.

The arrangement shown in these illustrations concentrates all the hand woodworking tools on the left-hand section of the backboard close to the vise. Auxiliary and metalworking tools such as wrenches and clamps are located on the right-hand section of the workbench, since these are used much less frequently. A small holder for paper toweling has been a recent addition on the right-hand end of the bench and this has also proved quite useful.

Another element that adds conveniences is the installation of electrical outlets in the backboard of the workbench. At first one outlet was installed in the left-hand side of the backboard. Over the years, the second outlet was added on the right-hand end of the workbench. The double outlets are quite convenient when the workbench is being shared by two generations each busy with his own style of project at opposite ends of the bench.

CONSTRUCTION OF THE WORKBENCH

The first step in construction is to cut the four vertical back beams. Holes should be drilled at the base of each beam, 34½ inches above the base and about 6 inches down from the top. The four beams should then be erected and bolted to the overhead beams of the house structure. The 34-inch long horizontal beams should then be cut and holes drilled 2 inches in from each end. These four beams may be assembled to the vertical beams if the rear bolts are drawn up very tight. The angle beams are cut 48 inches long with a hole drilled in 2 inches from each end. The diagonal beams are then bolted into place. Two legs 36 inches long are cut and bolted to two of the beams which run under the top of the workbench. A short "shelf support" 27 inches long is bolted to the back vertical beam and the leg. The 16-inch shelf is installed on top, and can be lightly nailed in place.

A 4 x 8-foot sheet of plywood ⅝-inch thick is purchased and cut 30 inches in from the long side. This gives two boards —one 30 inches by 8 feet and the other 18 inches by 8 feet. Small pads of ⅝-inch wood are installed on the back horizontal surfaces of the beams as filler blocks, then the workbench top is installed on the workbench and screwed down to the horizontal beams. This construction provides a plywood surface 1¼ inches thick in the front, where it takes a heavy beating, and ⅝-inch thick in the back, which takes less abuse.

The next step in building the workbench is to install the ¾-inch tongue-and-groove backboards on the vertical beams. Boards of any width may be used for backboards, or plywood may be selected. In the center of the backboard, an 18 x 18-inch set of shelves are installed. An appropriate opening should be left in the backboards for the shelves. The easiest construction is to subassemble a small box 6 inches deep by 18 inches wide and long, and fasten the shelves in the box. This subassembly may be pushed through the backboard opening and will remain in place due to gravity. For additional security the set of shelves may be held in place with one or two light screws.

The set of shelves are in a very convenient location to be reached from any working position on the bench. Useful small tools such as pencils, scribers, punches, knives are contained in small boxes on the top shelf of the inset cabinet. The most commonly used sizes of nails and screws are kept in glass jars on the shelves. Folding rulers and paper are kept on the upper surface of the inset box. These shelves are so handy that they will always be jammed with materials, but they provide much-needed storage in a convenient location.

Once the bench is completely assembled, it is a very good idea to put several coats of varnish on the top surface of the workbench and on the backboard. There is no need to finish any of the other surfaces, but heavy coats of varnish on the workbench top will aid greatly in keeping the surface clean. After the varnish dries, the vise and tools should be installed in their proper position.

2

Bedside Table

This bedside table is an excellent first project. It is simple in design and construction, and can be assembled from a wide variety of woods. The amount of wood required is small, and the cost of construction is relatively low. Best of all, the bedside table provides a handy piece of furniture which may be used in many different locations. The finished table is shown in FIGURE 1. The top shelf is an excellent height for a lamp for reading in bed. The upper shelf is large enough to hold a stack of exciting detective stories, or a clock-radio if you prefer listening to the latest music.

The bedside table is shown with the door open in FIGURE 2. The two lower shelves provide a handy storage space for a supply of books or magazines. Other things, such as binoculars or cameras may be kept out of sight on the lower shelves with the door closed. The combination of open and hidden storage allows a great deal of flexibility in the use of the table.

FASTENING WOODEN JOINTS

There is one fundamental problem in all furniture construction. This is the problem of how to join two pieces of wood at right angles to each other. This problem must be solved on even the simplest furniture. The easiest way to join two pieces

25

Figure 1

Figure 2

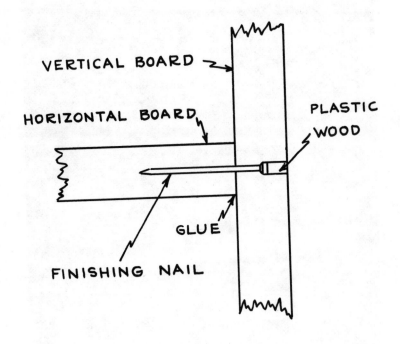

VERTICAL BOARD

HORIZONTAL BOARD

PLASTIC WOOD

FINISHING NAIL

GLUE

FIGURE 3

of wood is shown in FIGURE 3. The end of the horizontal board must be cut square and sanded smooth. Glue is smeared on the end of the wood and allowed to sink into the end grain. The location of the horizontal piece of wood should be scribed lightly on the vertical piece of wood. Glue should then be smeared on the vertical wood in between the two scribed lines. A second application of glue should be placed on the end of the horizontal board just before assembly. The boards are then placed in a proper position and several thin finishing nails driven in through the vertical piece into the horizontal piece of wood. Before the nails are driven flush with the surface of the vertical board stop hammering. Take a countersinking punch as shown in FIGURE 4 and place this carefully on the head of the nail. Strike the countersinking punch carefully with the hammer to drive the nails ⅛ to ¼ inch below the surface of the vertical board as shown in FIGURE 3. The open holes are then filled with plastic wood or a plug of solid wood.

This very simple method of joining was used on the bedside table. The combination of nails and glue has maintained strong and sturdy joints for 16 years of steady use. The disadvantage of this type of construction is that you can never get a perfect match between the plastic wood or wooden plug covering the head of the nail and the rest of the vertical board. Most people will never notice these small round plugs, but they are there and are visible if you look for them.

A second and stronger way of holding joints together is shown in FIGURE 5. Glue should be applied to the cut and sanded end of the horizontal board. The lines should again be scribed on the vertical board to give the exact placement of the horizontal boards. Glue should be placed on the vertical board in between the two scribed lines and a second coat placed on the end of the horizontal board. The horizontal board should then be held in place while a small drill is used to drill a hole through the vertical board and into the horizontal board. For a board 10 to 12 inches wide, two or three screws are usually sufficient. A larger drill should be placed in the chuck and the

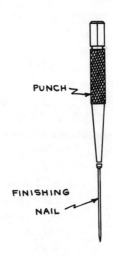

PUNCH

FINISHING
NAIL

FIGURE 4

holes in the vertical board should be enlarged. A "countersink-ing bit" should be placed in the drill and holes drilled in the vertical board to permit the head of the screw to sink well below the surface. If you do not have a countersink, then a 9/16-inch wood drill will do the job. The wood is assembled, and the screws driven in the joint and drawn up tight. As the screws are drawn up, glue will generally be forced out of the joint at both top and bottom. Casein glues are excellent for this type of work. They form a clear colorless material after

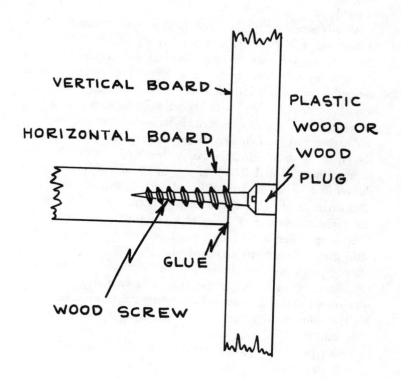

FIGURE 5

drying. The casein glues are water-soluble so that a wet rag may be used to remove the excess glue that has expanded out of the joint.

An advantage to the screwed joint is that it makes a very strong and rigid structure and is relatively simple to construct. A disadvantage is that the large diameter hole required to allow the head of the screw to be sunk below the surface is quite noticeable in the vertical piece of wood. The space above the screwhead must be filled with plastic wood or with a solid plug of wood which matches the remainder of the vertical board.

Another way to join two pieces of wood at right angles is shown in FIGURE 6. In this case a small filler strip about ¾ inches square is used. The first step in the assembly is to mark the position of the horizontal board on the vertical board. The filler strip should be cut to a length shorter than the width of the horizontal board. A series of holes are then drilled in the filler strip. Glue should be placed on one side of the filler strip and on the vertical board and the filler strip glued in place. Screws are then driven into the vertical board fastening the filler strip in its proper position. The final step is to place glue on the end and bottom of the horizontal board, and assemble the joint with vertical screws driven up through the filler strip into the horizontal board.

This type of glue joint provides large glue areas and a very sturdy construction without any screw holes showing in the exterior of the horizontal or vertical board. The disadvantage is that the end of the filler strip shows if the shelf or joint is exposed. This can often be minimized by placing the filler strip well back from the front of the horizontal board or by cutting a bevel angle on the filler strip so that it feathers out to a very thin board at the front of the piece of furniture.

Another way to make a blind joint is shown in FIGURE 7. A slot is cut in the vertical board ¼ to ⅜ inch deep. The end of the horizontal board is smeared with glue and glue is placed in the slot in the vertical board. The horizontal board is then driven in the slot and fine finishing nails driven in at an angle

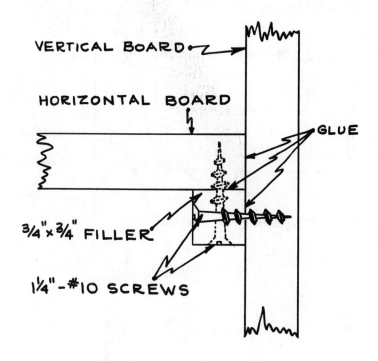

VERTICAL BOARD

HORIZONTAL BOARD

GLUE

¾" x ¾" FILLER

1¼"-#10 SCREWS

FIGURE 6

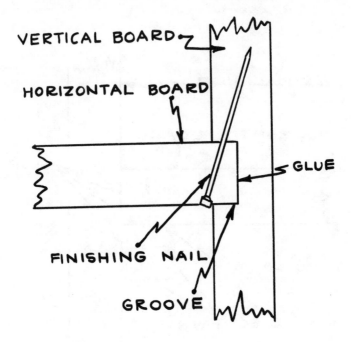

VERTICAL BOARD

HORIZONTAL BOARD

GLUE

FINISHING NAIL

GROOVE

FIGURE 7

up through the bottom of the horizontal board and into the vertical board. The finishing nails must be driven part way with the hammer and the remainder of the way with the punch or else you are almost certain to get hammer marks in the vertical board.

Another method of blind fastening is shown in FIGURE 8. It is extremely difficult to make a good sturdy joint by this method. In the first place, trying to drive the screw into the horizontal board almost invariably shifts its position. One way to hold it in place while the screw holes are being drilled and the screws driven is to clamp a back up board temporarily above the shelf to prevent any vertical motion of the board. The back up board is shown in dotted lines in FIGURE 8.

Another way to drill the holes is to clamp the horizontal board in a vise, and drill small holes in from the end. Then countersink the holes from the underside of the shelf.

In either case, the joint should be assembled with a back-up board clamped in place to prevent the shelf from shifting upward as the screws are drawn up tight. Do not overtighten the screws, or you are likely to split out a small section of wood below the screw. This method of construction using nails is not recommended.

Another simple method of joining is shown in FIGURE 9. Lines should be scribed on the vertical board to define the position of the horizontal board. A line should be drawn halfway between these two lines. Three holes should be drilled in the vertical board $\frac{1}{4}$ inch in diameter and about three quarters of the way through the vertical board. Lines should be scribed along the center of the horizontal board. Three $\frac{1}{4}$-inch holes should be drilled in this board with exactly the same spacing as the blind holes in the vertical board. Generally, it is well to drill these holes about 1 inch deep. Glue should be smeared on $\frac{1}{4}$-inch dowels and they should be driven into the holes in the horizontal board. The ends of the dowel should then be trimmed back to protrude slightly less than the depth of the blind holes in the vertical board between the lines, and the doweled

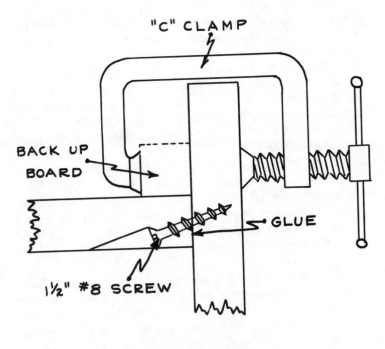

"C" CLAMP

BACK UP
BOARD

GLUE

1½" #8 SCREW

FIGURE 8

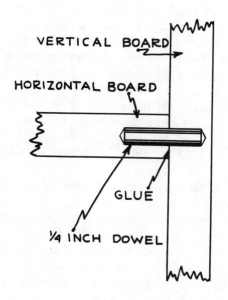

FIGURE 9

holes should be smeared with glue and the joint assembled with clamps.

In all cases, it is extremely important that when the joint is finished and the glue is still fresh the angle be checked to make sure that the two boards are at exactly right angles. A carpenter's square is an excellent tool to check the angle. Another way is to use a regular draftsman's T square. A third way is to cut the corner off a 4 x 8 sheet of plywood to make a large wooden triangle. Plywood is generally cut very square, but on some rare occasions the saw may cut a crooked sheet. It is well to have a friend check your homemade square with some kind of professional instrument. A large drafting triangle is another useful tool for checking angles.

CONSTRUCTION OF THE BEDSIDE TABLE

The design of the bedside table is shown in FIGURE 10 and FIGURE 12. Most of the table is made out of a 10-inch wide piece of No. 2 shelving. This is a very low cost material which is filled with knots. By careful selection at the lumber yard, you can find a piece of wood that has an interesting pattern and yet is not warped. Select the best seasoned wood you can find. The 10-inch wide board is actually 9⅝ inches wide after planing at the lumberyard. Saw the two sides and the three shelves directly from this first piece of wood. The sides are each 29¼ inches long. The three shelves should be cut 13⅛ inches long, and should then be planed or sawn to a width of 8¾ inches. Mark the position of each of the three shelves very carefully on the inside of the sideboards. A 17-inch length of 12-inch shelving is needed for the top. The bedside table was assembled using the glued joints shown in FIGURE 3 and this is the simplest type of joint to use for the first program. When the top, sides and shelves have all been cut and sanded to finished dimensions, these parts should be assembled as shown in the front view of FIGURE 10. The positioning of the top is shown in the side view of FIGURE 10.

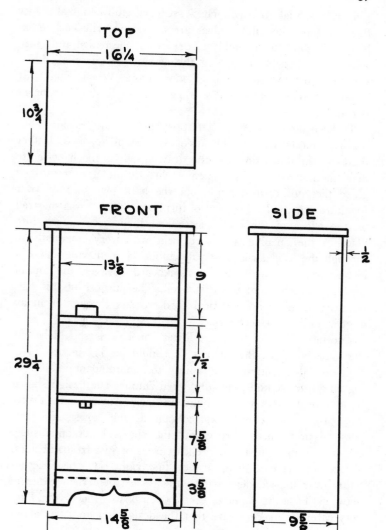

TOP

16¼

10¾

FRONT

13⅛

9

29¼

7½

7⅝

3⅝

14⅝

SIDE

½

9⅝

FIGURE 10

It is essential that you check very carefully to make sure that the top, sides and shelves are all square with each other before allowing the assembly to dry. With the nailed and glued joints it is possible to spring the assembly while the glue is wet to adjust for any small angular errors. When you finally have it set, completely square, then allow it to dry for one or two days.

To keep the early American appearance of the bedside table, the back pieces were made out of ⅜-inch plain wood. Rather than use the dimensions on the drawings, it is much better to take the dimensions of the opening directly off of your finished glued piece of furniture and cut the back pieces to fit your furniture exactly. In this piece of furniture, the glue was smeared on the edges of the back pieces and they were tapped into place in the opening and then held with very fine nails in through the sideboards. A small cutout ¾ inch wide and 2¼ inches long was made in the backboard between the top of the bedside table and the first shelf. The purpose of this cutout was to allow an electrical cord to pass through from an electric radio or electric clock.

The next piece to fit is the lower panel. This should be cut the same width as the shelves; it should be 3⅝ inches wide. You can allow your artistic ability to run rampant in designing an attractive and graceful curved cutout. The design shown in FIGURE 10 was very popular in early American furniture. The proportions can be varied considerably to satisfy your personal preferences. The cutout may be laid out on a sheet of paper using compasses, French curves or just freehand lines. When you have the appearance just right, lay the sheet of paper over the wooden board with a sheet of carbon paper in between. Tape the paper to the wooden board. Place your lines very carefully making sure that the design is symmetric about the center line.

If you have a jigsaw, it is a simple thing to cut out a curved surface. At the time this cabinet was constructed, no power tools were available. The curved surface was formed by making a

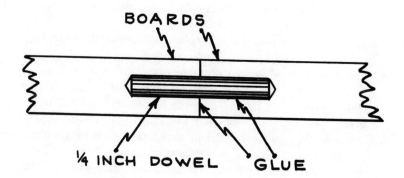

FIGURE 11

series of saw cuts into the penciled line as shown in the lower panel detail of FIGURE 12. The space between the cuts was carefully cut out with a wood chisel. The uneven surfaces were smoothed down with a rasp and filed to final shape with a smoother file. In doing work with either the chisel or the rasp, be very careful to always work from the front surface of the lower panel toward the back. Never reverse your stroke or there is a danger that you will split wood out of the front face of the lower panel.

The lower panel is then glued in place and held with small finishing nails going in through the sideboards.

The last piece to be added to the bedside table is the door. Construction details of the door are shown in FIGURE 12. Do not cut the door to the dimensions shown on the drawings. Measure the opening on your actual cabinet between the first shelf and the lowest shelf and between the sideboards. Subtract 1/16 inch from each of these dimensions and cut your door to this size. It is well to leave some extra material and remove the material slowly on final fitting particularly if this is your first woodworking project. The door on this cabinet was made from two pieces of wood which were glued together using a dowel joint as shown in FIGURE 11. The dowel joint is constructed with three or four 1/4-inch dowels. The joint should be well glued, and will be invisible on the finished piece. A small turned wooden drawer pull was fastened to one side of the door and decorative hinges were installed on the left-hand side. The actual hinges used in this bedside table were made up of standard brass hinges with 1/8-inch-thick solid brass decorative panels added to each side. These were sawn and filed by hand to finished shape since satisfactory decorative hinges were not available 16 years ago. Now, attractive antique hinges in many different patterns and styles are available, and should be chosen for installation on the bedside table. A spring clip or magnetic catch should be installed on the back side of the door and on the underside of the second shelf to provide a means for holding the door shut.

LOWER PANEL DETAIL

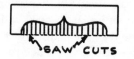

SAW CUTS

SECTION OF TABLE

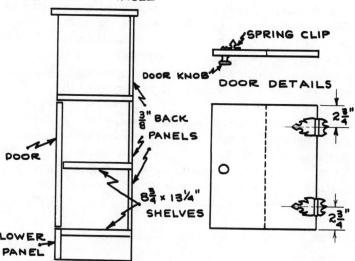

SPRING CLIP

DOOR KNOB

DOOR DETAILS

DOOR

3/8" BACK PANELS

8 3/4 x 13 1/4" SHELVES

LOWER PANEL

2 3/4"

2 3/4"

FIGURE 12

Small furniture gliders may be installed on the bottom of the two sides of the bedside table. These make it easier to move the table around, but are not really necessary.

FINISHING OPERATIONS

After the bedside table is completely assembled, all of the exterior surfaces should be sanded to a smooth surface. You will normally find cracks and checks around the knotholes and these should be filled with plastic wood and sanded to a smooth surface. Surfaces should be sanded either by hand or with a belt type or vibrating sander. Do not use any rotary sanding device because this will place cuts in the wood crosswise to the grain and these cuts are extremely difficult to remove.

On this bedside table a simple finishing technique was used which is a good choice for a first project. The entire table was stained using a maple stain. The stain should be applied with a brush and allowed to remain for ten minutes and then the excess removed with a rag. Follow the directions on the manufacturer's label very carefully. If the first coat is not deep enough, add another coat later on, but leave the material on less time before rubbing off. After staining this bedside table was finished with many, many coats of furniture paste wax. Such a finish is strong and durable and is simple to apply. All it requires is lots of wax and lots of elbow grease. Put on a coat of wax twice a day for a week and you will build up a tough and durable surface.

3

Mahogany Bookcase

Another project using the same basic techniques is a mahogany bookcase. The author and his wife designed and built two such bookcases which have been useful and attractive additions in the living rooms of our homes for ten years. The finished appearance of the bookcase is shown in FIGURE 1.

Tall books are kept on their side on the bottom shelf. Books up to 11½ inches high may be placed on the second shelf, while

Figure 1

books up to 9½ inches high will fit on the top shelf. The shelf spacing may be shifted to suit the needs of the books in your library. The bookcases were constructed from solid Philippine Mahogany lumber purchased from an area lumberyard.

For this bookcase, the mahogany boards were planed to an even 1-inch thickness and to even widths of 12 and 15 inches by the lumberyard. In order to secure boards to these even dimensions, it is necessary to purchase boards which are 1¼ inches thick by 13 or 16 inches wide in the rough sawn shape. Most lumberyards will then plane them to the exact thickness you desire. If you cannot get this heavy material, the bookcase may be made out of standard 1-inch planks. The 1-inch material is generally 13/16 inch thick after it is planed to finished dimensions. Other woods such as cherry, pine, maple or walnut may be used. If wide planks are not available, then the widths must be made up from two pieces using the edge gluing method shown in FIGURE 11 of Chapter 2.

The wood required for each bookcase includes:

Top—Plank with 34 inches of perfect wood 15 inches wide. (A plank about 42 inches should be purchased and the ends trimmed off.)

Sides and Shelves—14-foot plank with a finished width of 12 inches.

Front Panel—3 x 32 inches.

Back Panel—3/16 inch or ¼-inch mahogany plywood 31 inches by 27½ inches.

Note: The *top,* one *shelf,* and the *front panel* may be cut from a plank 6 feet long and 15 inches wide. The remaining two *shelves* and the *sides* may be cut from a board 11 feet long by 12 inches wide.

The two shelves in the bookcase are completely removable and add no structural strength to the construction. The bookcase is built as a great big open box. In order to strengthen the corner joints, the construction shown in FIGURE 6 of Chapter 2 was used. One-half inch by ¾-inch mahogany corner pieces were installed between the sideboards and the top shelf and the sideboards and the bottom shelf. These reinforcements plus a screwed on backboard give a very rigid and durable structure.

The first step in construction is to lay out the side panels on the 12-inch wide board. Two side panels are cut each 29½ inches long. It is important to cut off a short distance at the end of the plank to remove any checks or discolored surface. Be careful that the end cut is square with the long edge of the plank. It is well to set the square on the top surface of the wood as the sawing is done to be sure that the crosscut saw is cutting exactly vertically through the wood. When the first cut is finished lay off two lengths of 29½ inches each and make these two cuts as carefully as possible.

The next step is to cut a 34-inch length from the widest plank for the *top*. By the time the bookcases were constructed, I had access to a circular saw with a set of molding cutters. A scalloped cutter was used to provide a simple rounded shape on the edge of the *top* board as shown in the detail of FIGURE 2.

Molding cutters are rather dangerous to use and you should be very careful with safety precautions. Most cutter heads have provision for three inserted blades. Be sure the blades are fully seated and locked tightly in place with the set screws.

It is well to practice on many scraps of lumber before making a molding cut on your expensive piece of wood. Even with the greatest care, you will find a lot of fine ripples in the wood after the cuts are finished. No matter how bad they look, do not try to recut the same surface a second time. This procedure will almost invariably make the surface look worse and may irrevocably ruin the piece of wood.

Feed the wood through the molding cutters slowly and very carefully, making sure that the wood is held vertical in relation to the work table of the circular saw. When one cut is finished, proceed to the next cut.

The best way to touch up imperfections is to use a block of wood with sandpaper wrapped around it. You cannot make it perfect so don't worry about it. Make it as smooth and even as possible by hand finishing.

The next step is to select the better of the two long surfaces and place this towards the front of the bookcase. Feel confident that no one but you will ever know how many small nicks and gouges were actually made in the surface.

Three shelves should be cut from the 12-inch-wide plank of wood. The lowest shelf should be 29½ inches long and the middle two shelves should be 29¼ inches long. The two middle shelves should be set to one side until the bookcase is finished. Next, cut four small strips of wood ½ inch thick by ¾ inch wide by 10½ inches long. The installation of the strips is shown in the front view and the Section A-A of FIGURE 2. The corner strip is perforated like a piece of Swiss cheese with three screw holes drilled horizontally and three holes drilled vertically along the length of the strip. Smear the corner strips with glue and screw them firmly to the sides of the bookcase at the top, and in position to hold the lower shelf.

Next, fasten the top in place. Glue should be smeared on the wood surfaces which contact the top and then the screws should be driven vertically up through the corner strip into the top surface. Be sure that the screws are a proper length to get a good grip in the wood, but not project through the upper surface of the top. The bottom shelf should then be fastened in place using exactly the same technique.

After the joints are made and screwed up tight, check to make sure the sides, top and bottom shelf are exactly square with each other. If they are not quite square, it is possible to force the surfaces slightly. In an extreme case, it may be necessary to use a clamp or wedges to hold the bookcase in an exactly square position while the back panel is installed.

The back panel can be made out of 3/16-inch or ¼-inch plywood. It is well to get plywood which has mahogany on one surface to match the remainder of the bookcase. The back should be cut 31 inches long so that it sets in from the sides ¼ inch on each side. Glue should be smeared on the sides

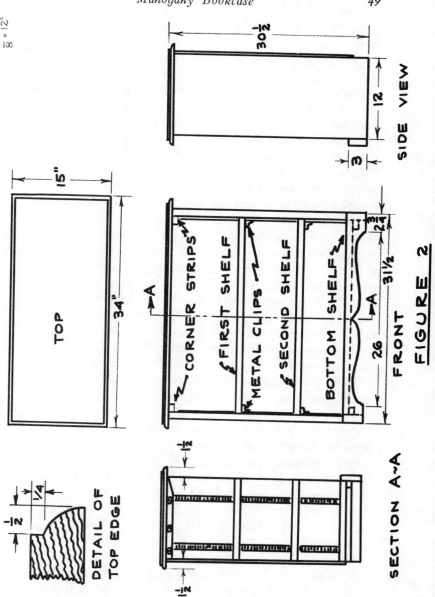

FIGURE 2

and on the bottom shelf and the back fastened to the sides and bottom shelf with screws.

The assembly should be checked once more to make sure all the surfaces are square and then set aside to dry for two days.

The decorative cuts on the front panel give you an area for artistic expression. The top of the front panel should be flush with the lower shelf. Any design may be used which you feel is artistically suitable. The design shown in these illustrations is a popular one on early American cabinet work. The design should be laid out carefully on a sheet of paper and then transferred to the wood using carbon paper.

One trick to make sure that the design is exactly symmetric is to draw up only one half of the design. Mark the center line of your wooden front panel and the center line of the design. Then transfer one half the design to the wood using a sheet of carbon paper. The design will be quite clearly outlined on the reverse side of the sheet of paper after the transfer. The design may then be flipped over and transferred to the other side of the front panel. The shape may be cut out using a hand jigsaw, a power jigsaw or with the handsaw and chisel technique described in Chapter 2. The front panel is then fastened to the lower shelf and the side using small corner strips on the vertical and horizontal surfaces.

The bookcase is designed so that the first and second shelves may be moved vertically. Perforated metal tracks can be purchased which are easily fastened to the sides in the position shown in Section A-A of FIGURE 2. The shelves are held in a vertical position by small metal clips which snap through holes in the metal track. It is necessary to cut small notches in the first and second shelves to allow clearance for the metal tracks.

FINISHING THE BOOKCASE

When the bookcase is all glued together and the shelves fitted in place, it should be sanded using medium and then fine sandpaper. Hidden fasteners are used throughout so that there are no screw heads or nail heads to be covered up with plastic wood. The corner strips beneath the top surface are invisible since the eye is normally higher than the top of the bookcase. Even if you lean down to remove a book from the shelf, the corner strip is in deep shadow and will not be noticed.

The bookcase was first finished with a mixture of 50 per cent varnish and 50 per cent turpentine. Put this on as a thin coat so that there are no drip marks on the sides. After the first coat has dried, the grain of the wood will have raised in small ridges. This should be rubbed down with fine sandpaper and a second coat of the mixture applied. The wood should be rubbed down a second time with very fine sandpaper and a third coat of the thin mixture applied.

After the third coat, rub the wooden surfaces down with steel wool and apply a very thin coat of full strength varnish. Keep adding thin coats of varnish with the steel wool treatment after each coat until either your patience or the varnish runs out.

Mahogany is a fairly open grained wood and a number of coats of varnish are required to fully seal the pores and give an even, smooth finish. Mahogany is an excellent wood for construction projects of this type, since it is relatively inexpensive and generally has beautiful coloring and grain. The relatively porous grain structure makes it easy to work, but requires that many coats of finish be applied to fully seal the wood.

The bookcase loaded with its usual assortment of books is shown in FIGURE 3. Large books are stored horizontally on the lowest shelf. Books up to 11½ inches high will fit on the middle shelf, and books 9½ inches or less will fit on the upper shelf.

These bookcases have proved to be very useful and attractive pieces of furniture. When placed next to your favorite chair, and a large lamp set on top, you are all set for months of enjoyable reading. The top surface has ample space for an ash tray and a stack of magazines to further occupy those long winter evenings.

Figure 3

4

Casting Light on the Subject

Once you have fabricated several pieces of furniture such as bookcases and bedside tables, you will have an urgent need for lamps. Three different types of lamps are described in this chapter and the techniques of construction may be applied to a wide range of other materials. The simplest type of lamp is one made from a tall cylindrical brass object. Such a lamp made from an old 37mm artillery shell is shown in FIGURE 1. Old empty cartridge cases of this type are sometimes found in antique shops, Army-Navy stores or military surplus stores. They usually are a dark greenish brown and dented. Since the brass sides are heavy, it is well to skip any case which is badly bent. Any other objects with a relatively small cylindrical mouth can be turned into a lamp by the same construction technique. This includes old copper and brass pitchers, antique bottles, and similar objects. A large pitcher which was made into a lamp is shown in FIGURE 3 of Chapter 3.

The first step in construction is to place a large iron bar into the vise on your workbench. The iron bar should be as close in diameter to the mouth of the cartridge case as possible. The cartridge case should be rotated gently and the dents hammered out by pounding with a hard rubber mallet. Care must be taken in pounding since the hammer marks may be more objectionable than the original dents. If a series of fine marks appear around the dented portion, the hammer is too hard.

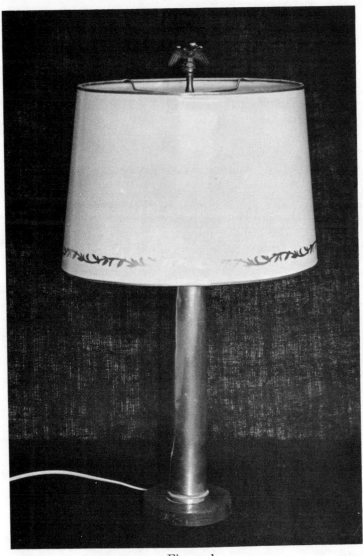

Figure 1

The next step is to get a powerful brass cleaner. Some of the new chemical cleaners remove discoloration rapidly. If it is necessary to use more vigorous means, stay with a very fine abrasive. Do not use anything coarser than a pad of steel wool and soap. Anything as coarse as sandpaper or emery cloth will leave a network of fine lines which are almost impossible to remove.

Some authorities recommend spraying polished brass or copper surfaces with several coats of clear lacquer. The problem with this approach is that eventually the lacquer flakes off in some areas and the brass begins to take on a very patchy look. In order to restore the luster, you are faced with the problem of removing all the rest of the lacquer before the brass can be repolished. Removal of the remaining lacquer can be a very difficult and time-consuming job.

A better approach is to leave the brass uncovered. If it is left alone, it will gradually darken into deeper and deeper tones of yellow. If it becomes discolored from many small sticky fingerprints, the brass may be repolished with a chemical cleaner without disassembling the lamp.

The construction details of this type of lamp are shown in FIGURE 2. The base was made by cutting a 5-inch circle from mahogany wood ¾ inch thick. Two lamps were made to exactly the same pattern and the bases were sawn out by hand. The bases do not have to be exactly round to make very acceptable lamps. Minor imperfections can be smoothed with a file, and a block of wood covered with medium sandpaper. The upper edge of the base should be rounded slightly, to give a smooth appearance.

A 3/16-inch hole is drilled in the base of the old cartridge case or through the bottom of the brass pitcher or whatever other object you are using. *Be absolutely sure* that the primer of the cartridge case has been fired before drilling. If you are in doubt, consult someone who has been in the Armed Services and can advise you. Fasten the brass case to the wooden base using a large diameter wood screw as shown on the right side

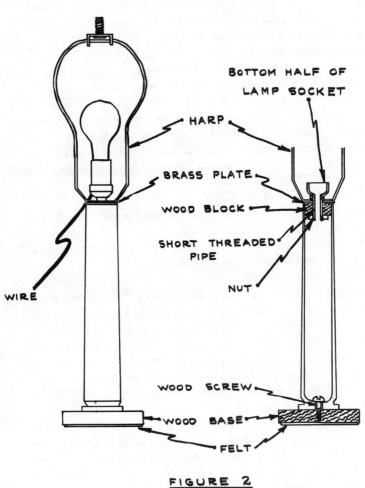

FIGURE 2

of FIGURE 2. Glue a circle of cloth to the bottom of the wooden base in order to protect the funiture. Casein glue is an excellent way to attach the cloth to the bottom of the base.

The neck of the old shell should be measured very carefully and a wooden plug cut to be very slightly larger, so that it is a tight fit. Purchase the lamp socket, harp, a short nipple, and a nut at a lamp shop or hardware store. Cut a small sheet of brass 1/16 inch to ⅛ inch thick to the same diameter as the outside of the mouth of the shell case. Purchase a light socket with a hole in the side to allow the wire to come out the base of the socket as shown in FIGURE 2. If you cannot find sockets of this design, then drill a 3/16-inch-diameter hole to allow the wire to pass through.

The next step is to assemble the upper parts as shown in the cross-section drawing on the right side of FIGURE 2. Screw the short nipple into the lower half of the lamp socket. Then assemble the harp, the brass disk, the wooden plug and finally draw the assembly up tight with a nut. Set this assembly on the top of the lamp and gently drive it down into place using a wooden dowel to push on the inside of the lower half of the lamp socket. Then the electrical wiring should be completed. The final steps are to screw in an electric light bulb and attach an attractive shade to the upper surface of the harp. The shade is held on with an ornamental brass nut, or finial, which screws on to the upper bracket on the harp, thus holding the shade firmly in place.

PISTOL LAMP

An old pistol may be put on display in a novel and effective way by making it into a table lamp. The only alteration needed on most guns is one hole through the frame at the heel of the grip. If you don't have a pistol to use, a suitable one can often be found at antique stores or in a gunsmith's scrap pile. The gun is for decoration only so it does not need to work or even have all its parts. I have made two such lamps. One was made from the frame of a .36 caliber Whitney revolver which was bought in an antique store in New Orleans minus the entire cylinder and cylinder pin assembly. A perfectly satisfactory lamp was made by turning up a dummy cylinder from a large bar of cold rolled steel, and making a dummy cylinder pin out of a smaller piece of cold rolled steel.

A second lamp was made from a .31 caliber Whitney revolver which was missing all of its internal mechanism. This lamp is shown in FIGURE 3. A crude trigger was sawn and filed to shape out of cold rolled steel and a new weak hammer spring was made out of brass to hold the hammer up in its proper position in the revolver.

To start the lamp, take a 12-inch-wide piece of clear pine or mahogany about ¾ inch thick and scribe an 8-inch-diameter circle on the better side. Cut this out on a band saw or as closely as possible with a handsaw. A sharp plane will bring the base very closely to a circle, and it may be made round by filing or electric sanding. The top of the base should be rounded using the plane and then sanding to make a surface that will not show nicks or dents easily. Give the base several coats of stain if it is pine or several coats of varnish if it is mahogany. In either case the base should be given several coats of wax after finishing to make a tough durable finish. Then put the base to one side until your pistol is ready for mounting.

The electric cord for the lamp may be run down inside the barrel and right on down through the cylinder and out the space between the end of cylinder and the frame where the cartridge head fits. This may be done on old revolvers by forcing the cylinder as far forward as possible. If a little additional space is needed, hacksaw and file a shallow groove in the end of the chamber. Do not use this approach if it is a valuable pistol. If you are fitting a dummy cylinder, it is easier to cut the groove at the barrel end of the cylinder. It is only necessary to drill the chambers ¼ inch to ½ inch deep to

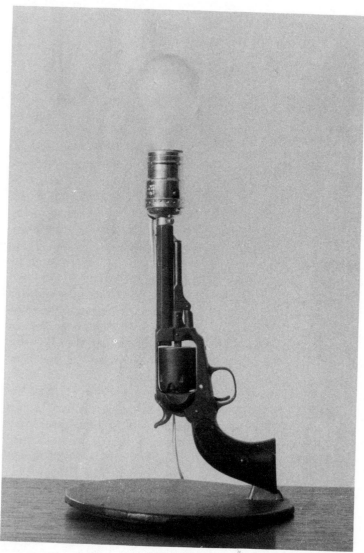

Figure 3

achieve a realistic appearance. Another way to construct the lamp is to run the wire out through the side of the lamp socket, as shown in FIGURE 4. This approach is simple, and minimizes changes to the firearm.

To support the pistol on its base, a small lead casting is required. A mold may easily be made by tacking short pieces of wood onto a plank and using the frame itself as the upper part of the casting as shown in FIGURE 5. Scrap lead such as old automobile tire weights are excellent material for they melt at a low temperature and may be melted in a little tin can over a gas flame. Pour plenty of lead into the mold as the lead has a tendency to sink in the center. If too much is cast, the excess may always be filed off. File the casting to a clean surface, and drill a 3/16-inch hole on the center line as shown in FIGURE 5. Hold the lead casting against the frame of the revolver, and run a 3/16-inch drill up through the hole in the lead to mark the proper hole location on the frame of the revolver. The hole through the frame of the revolver can be slightly smaller such as 5/32 inch in diameter.

The next step is to set the casting and pistol on the wooden base with the vertical barrel as close to the center of the base circle as possible. Remove the pistol, and spot the position of the hole through the lead casting into the wood base. Drill the hole through the wooden base and then recess the underside of the base so that the head of the bolt will be flush with the undersurface, and not mar any furniture that it is placed on. The frame of the pistol should be left in an antique brown finish, and not polished up and re-blued. If there are bright spots on the frame, a "cold blueing," material may be used to reduce the shine. The cold blueing is also excellent for repairing bright spots on gun parts with a blued finish. "Cold blueing" is available at many stores that sell firearms.

A cross section of the lamp assembly is shown in FIGURE 4. The first step in assembly is to put a long bolt up through the base, lead casting and frame of the revolver. A small triangular washer on the inside of the gun frame is helpful to prevent the

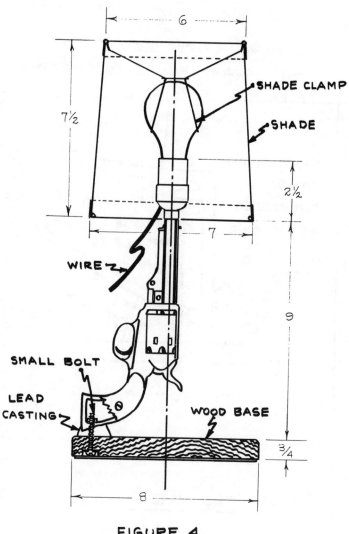

6

7½

2½

7

9

¾

8

SHADE CLAMP

SHADE

WIRE

SMALL BOLT

LEAD
CASTING

WOOD BASE

FIGURE 4

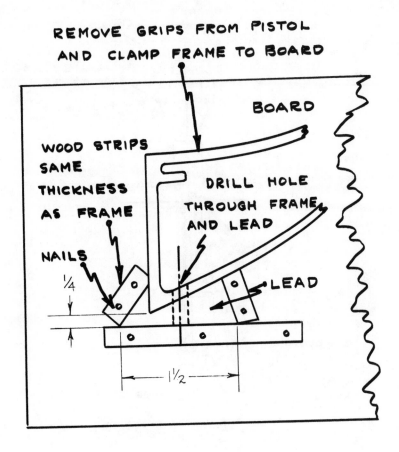

REMOVE GRIPS FROM PISTOL
AND CLAMP FRAME TO BOARD

BOARD

WOOD STRIPS
SAME
THICKNESS
AS FRAME

DRILL HOLE
THROUGH FRAME
AND LEAD

NAILS

¼

LEAD

1½

FIGURE 5

bolt from bending. Tighten the bolt up firmly to prevent wobbling. The revolver grips may then be replaced.

Purchase an electric socket and a short pipe extension to fit it. The extension must fit snugly into the barrel of the pistol and this may be accomplished by filing if it is too large, or wrapping with thin sheet metal if it is too small. Drive the extension in carefully to avoid marring the upper threads. Hold the pistol in one hand while doing this or the base will certainly be damaged. Screw the socket onto the extension. Next, run the wire down through the socket down through the barrel and through the cylinder of the gun feeding it out carefully through the opening at the lower end of the revolver. On some guns it is necessary to feed the wire up through the opening through the cylinder and this you will have to experiment with for your particular gun. Put the plug on one end on the electric wire and finish wiring up the socket at the other end. For these small lamps, "clamp on" shades were used. These shades are constructed with two spring fingers which grip the light bulb directly.

The finished lamp is shown in FIGURE 6. This type of lamp provides an interesting method for displaying a small link with the history of America. You will see the lamp and enjoy it far more than if it was hidden away in some dark cabinet. Do not mutilate a pistol which is in good working order, because old pistols of this type are becoming more and more valuable. The pistol lamp provides particularly appropriate light for reading adventure stories of the Old West.

TALL STANDING LAMP

A rifle or shotgun too old for shooting may be utilized in a very decorative and useful way by converting it into a floor lamp. The rifle shown in these illustrations was an old single-shot rifle manufactured in the late nineteenth century. Numerous rifles of this type are available at low cost, particularly

Figure 6

if too worn for further shooting. These rifles may be found in antique stores, military surplus stores, or some sporting goods stores. The old black-powder rifles are generally chambered for obsolete cartridges, and are suitable for decoration only. They are normally priced below $15. The older rifles have long barrels of 28 to 34 inches, and they can be converted into a lamp about 5 feet high which is an excellent height for a reading lamp. The appearance of the finished lamp is shown in FIGURE 7. An old shotgun may also be used, but this will generally result in a lamp about 12 inches lower. Construction details of the rifle lamp are shown in FIGURE 8.

The first step in making a lamp is to glue together two 8-inch-wide by ¾-inch-thick boards edge to edge for the base. Use two pieces each about 17 inches long and glue them together using four ⅜-inch dowels. When the glue has dried, the base can be hand sawed or band sawed to a circular shape. The upper edge should be rounded so that it is resistant to nicks and scratches. The base of this lamp was cut with a hand saw and then rounded with a rasp. This method is recommended if power tools are not available.

The next item is a base block for the butt of the rifle. This piece of wood should fit the contour of the stock of the rifle with the buttplate removed. It needs to be thicker at the toe of the stock than at the heel so that the barrel of the rifle stands vertically when mounted on the lamp base. The best way to make the base block is to remove the buttplate from the stock of the rifle and use it as a template to outline the proper contour on a piece of ¾-inch-thick wood.

Cut out the contour using hand tools or a jigsaw, and file the surface of the base block to match the contour on the butt end of the rifle. The shape should be filed until the barrel of the rifle stands vertically. When the base block is located so that the barrel of the rifle stands over the exact center of the circular base, then remove the rifle and mark the position of the base block carefully on the circle of wood. Two holes should be drilled down through the base block and through the base

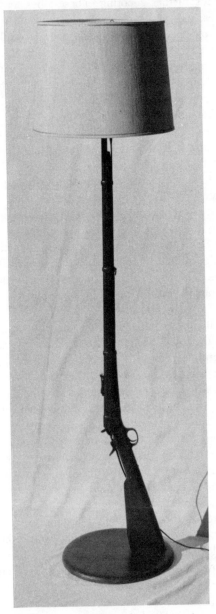

Figure 7

of the lamp. These holes should be lined up with the buttplate screw holes in the rifle if possible. The base can then be finished with a dark brown stain to match the rifle stock and completed with several coats of wax for protection.

The rifle is assembled to the base by driving two large wood screws up through the wooden base, and the base block, and into the buttstock of the rifle. This detail is shown in the lower part of FIGURE 8.

The construction of the upper part of the lamp is very similar to that used in the pistol lamp. Because the lamp is much larger and more powerul, a three-way 100-200-300-watt socket was selected and an 8-inch frosted glass bowl. A 1-inch-long pipe extension ½ inch in diameter fits half into the porcelain fixture and half into the barrel of the rifle. With a rifle barrel under .50 caliber, the pipe extension should be filed down for half its length so that it is a tight drive fit in the barrel. A larger barrel, such as on a shotgun, requires a separate plug which is a tight fit in the bore. It is very important that it be a tight drive fit in the barrel of the firearm.

A piece of two-conductor wire 10 feet long should be cut and threaded down through the upper part of the pipe extension down through the barrel and out through the action of the rifle as shown in FIGURE 8. An electric plug can then be attached to the exposed end. If you want to get really fancy, a long hole may be drilled through the buttstock of the rifle and the wire can be fed down through the action through the buttstock and out the base of the lamp. With most of the old rifles, it is much simpler to run the wire out through the action where the cartridge fits.

About 7 inches of wire should be left projecting above the pipe in the top of the barrel. A small lock nut should be screwed down on the pipe extension as far as possible. The sheet metal outer covering to the electric socket should be placed over the pipe. The ends of the wire should be bared and attached to the terminals on the porcelain socket. The socket is then screwed down tight on the pipe extension, and a glass

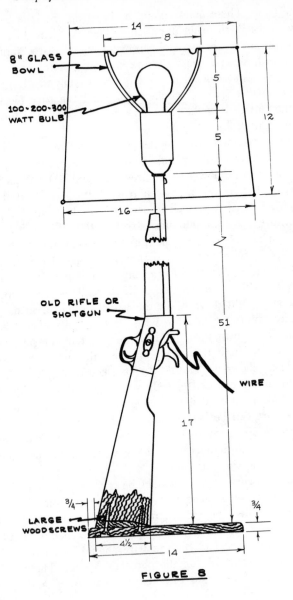

8" GLASS BOWL

100-200-300 WATT BULB

OLD RIFLE OR SHOTGUN

WIRE

LARGE WOODSCREWS

FIGURE 8

bowl set on top of the fixture. The addition of a three-way bulb and a shade complete the project. The shade used in the lamp illustrated is 16 inches wide at the bottom and 12 inches high and of a white parchment-type plastic material which softens the glare without cutting down the amount of light available. This type of lamp lends itself to all kinds of fancy shades, if you are so inclined. This lamp was first constructed twenty years ago, and has outlasted many shades. One interesting shade was a leather shade sewn with rawhide, which gave a frontier appearance to the lamp.

The lamp is attractive and durable, and provides an interesting conversation piece as well as providing excellent illumination beside your favorite chair in the living room or den.

5

High-Fidelity Cabinet

This high-fidelity cabinet is designed so that many different types of high fidelity components may be installed. The assembled cabinet, with the doors open, is shown in FIGURE 1. A wide variety of amplifiers may be installed on the upper shelf of the right-hand side and many different models of phonograph turntables may be installed in the compartment in the upper left-hand side of the cabinet.

The arrangement shown in FIGURE 1 permits storage of ap-

Figure 1

proximately 220 12-inch long-playing records in the cardboard jackets in seven separate compartments. The storage space may also be used to store four hundred 45 rpm records without any dust jackets. The inclusion of seven different compartments gives ample space for classical music for the adults at one end, musical comedy and other light records in the middle, and the all out modern popular music for the youngsters at the other end of the storage space.

ALTERNATE DESIGN OF CABINET

The high-fidelity cabinet may also be constructed so that all of the space on the right side of the center wall is filled with electronic equipment. With this arrangement, there is sufficient space for about 125 long-playing records in their cardboard jackets or 230 popular records without jackets. Three shelves may be installed to take an AM tuner, an FM tuner, and an amplifier. Short-wave tuners or a tape equipment shelf may be substituted, based on your particular interest. The actual positioning of these shelves will be determined by the height of the electronic components that you purchase. If you choose this configuration, it is a good idea to leave the back completely off the cabinet on this side in order to encourage air circulation. High-powered electronic components can develop a great deal of heat and large ¾-inch or 1-inch holes should be drilled through each of the three shelves in order to allow vertical air circulation up through the shelves and the electronic equipment.

This particular cabinet has been in use for ten years. It was originally constructed with the right side reserved for electronic equipment. Recently, the monaural amplifier and record changer were replaced with stereo equipment of different design. Changing equipment is quite simple and requires only cutting out a new front panel to fit the new amplifier, and the construction of a new cutout board of ¼-inch plywood to properly support the new record changer design.

The dimensions of the cabinet are shown in FIGURE 2. The

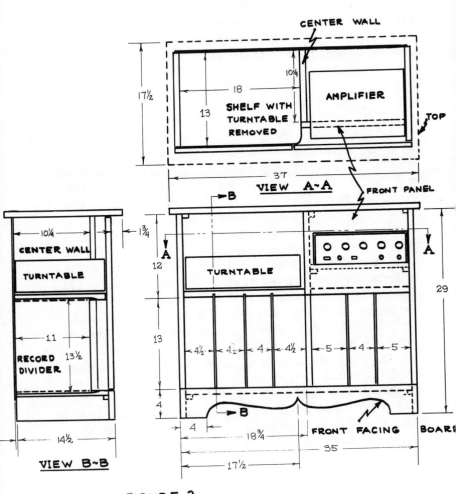

FIGURE 2

major components of the cabinet were made from two planks of mahogany. One was an extra wide plank 18 inches wide by 1 inch thick by 14 feet long. The following pieces were cut from this board: *Top* 37 inches long, two *doors* each 24¾ inches long, and a *bottom shelf* from the remainder of this section of the plank which ended up 13½ inches wide and 33 inches long.

In the original construction, another section of this wide board was cut 25 inches long by 15 inches wide. This was mounted as the *front panel* with the grain running vertically on the right-hand side of the cabinet with the intention of hav- the amplifier in the upper section and an AM tuner, and a FM tuner in the lower section. If you plan to mount more than one piece of electronic equipment in the hi-fi cabinet, it is well to follow this plan which gives ample room for three shelves of electronic equipment if needed.

The second piece of wood required for the cabinet is a plank 11 or 12 feet long by 14 inches wide by 1 inch thick. This plank will have finished dimensions of 13½ inches wide by 13/16 inches thick. The two *sides* of the cabinet each 29 inches long should be cut from this plank. The *center wall* which forms the center partition of the cabinet and a *horizontal shelf* on which the phonograph rests are also cut from this piece of wood. The box on which the phonograph turntable rests is also cut from this plank.

The first step in construction is to cut the top, the two sides, the vertical internal partition, and the two horizontal shelves. If you wish to have record storage space all across the bottom of the cabinet as shown in FIGURE 1, then a series of five grooves must be cut into the top surface of the lower shelf. Each of these grooves is ⅛ inch wide by about ¼ inch deep. Matching grooves should be cut in the underside of the middle shelf on which the turntable box is mounted.

The first elements to be assembled are the top, sides, and lower shelf. These four parts more or less form a large open box. The joints are assembled using the construction shown

in FIGURE 6 of Chapter 2. Three-quarter inch by ¾-inch mahogany strips were placed in the interior corners to make very
strong joints. Three of the four corner strips are completely
hidden when the construction is finished, and the fourth one
is almost impossible to see. Be very sure that the joints are
exactly square before allowing the glue to completely dry.

One way to hold the parts in proper alignment is to cut
the back panel from 3/16-inch plywood 25¾ inches wide by
34 inches long and temporarily screw this in place to hold the
tops and sides exactly perpendicular with each other. After
these components have thoroughly dried, the next step is to fit
the internal shelves and partitions. The center wall is placed
in first. It is positioned at the upper surface where it butts
the top with a ¾ x ¾-inch corner filler. At the bottom the
partition is held in place by screws up through the lower shelf.
The horizontal shelves are then placed in the cabinet. The
shelf on the left-hand side should be mahogany 13½ inches
wide. The center partition is only 11 inches wide and the shelf
on the right-hand side should only be 11 inches wide. This
difference in dimensions is important to allow the face panel
which covers the amplifier to be set in several inches from
the front of the cabinet. This space is important to allow room
for the knobs on the amplifier and other electronic equipment
when the doors of the cabinet are shut. The set back of the
front panel is shown in View A-A of FIGURE 2.

With the horizontal shelves in place, the next step is to cut
the dividers for the record compartments from ⅛-inch ma-
sonite or plywood. Five dividers are required. These should
be slid in place from the back of the cabinet and generally
do not require any kind of fastening.

The next step is to construct a small box to hold the phonograph turntable or automatic record changer. The details of
this box are shown in FIGURE 3. There is enough wood to
cut the front and the two sides from one 17-inch length of
the very wide mahogany board. The back of the box may
be made from any type of wood that is available. The box is

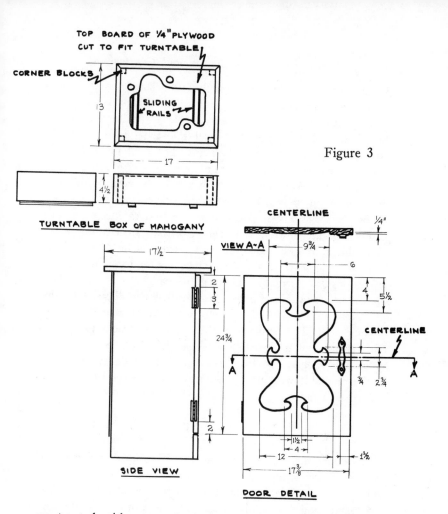

TOP BOARD OF ¼" PLYWOOD
CUT TO FIT TURNTABLE

CORNER BLOCKS

13

17

SLIDING RAILS

Figure 3

4½

TURNTABLE BOX OF MAHOGANY

CENTERLINE

¼"

VIEW A-A

9¾

17½

6

2

3

4

5½

24¾

A

A

CENTERLINE

A

A

¾

2¾

2

1½

4

12

1½

17⅜

SIDE VIEW

DOOR DETAIL

constructed with supporting corner fillers which come up to ¼-inch below the upper surface on the inside. A sheet of plywood with mahogany facing on one side should be cut to fit the upper opening of the box.

When you purchase a turntable or an automatic record changer, a paper template will be included somewhere in the packaging. This paper template should be laid over the ¼ inch thick mahogany board and a cutout shape scribed onto the plywood. This shape must then be cut out using hand saw,

jig saw, or saber saw. The template will show the critical locations for spring mounting and other things required for
your particular design of turntable. It is recommended that
the ¼ inch plywood merely be set into the top of the mahogany box, but not fastened in place. This will make it easier
to remove the entire assembly for servicing and makes it easier
to replace the record changer with a more modern or different
model as your tastes and interests change.

The turntable box is installed in the hi-fi cabinet as a completely separate unit. It is mounted on two steel tracks which
allow the unit to be slid out some seven inches towards the
front of the cabinet to allow easier access for changing records
or cleaning the turntable. The record changer is normally kept
all the way towards the back of the cabinet. Tracks of this
type are generally available in stores specializing in high-fidelity equipment. The addition of these movable tracks is a desirable feature, but it is really not essential. Most modern turntables are designed so that the records may be easily placed
on the turntable without the need to move the entire assembly
out to the front.

DOORS AND FITTINGS

The doors for the hi-fi cabinet are 17⅜ inches wide by almost 24¾ inches high. Each was made from one piece of the
wide mahogany plank. The two doors are identical in size
and design, and differ only in the placement of hinges and door
pull. The appearance of the cabinet with the doors closed is
shown in FIGURE 4. The fronts of the doors were hand carved
with a relief pattern of an early American design.

The carving was done using very sharp knives and chisels
and it is about ⅛ inch deep at the edges. Antiqued copper hardware was used with the cabinet, such as hinges and door pulls.
The one-piece solid doors give a beautifully matching pattern
of wood, but it is really preferable to make the front door
panels out of two to three pieces of mahogany edge glued to-

Figure 4

gether. The reason is that a single piece of wood will tend to warp all in one direction, while several pieces laminated together have a better chance of holding their proper shape.

The design of the door is shown in FIGURE 3. The pattern selected combines elements of several early American designs into a symmetric and pleasing pattern. This is a place where you can express your own artistic ideas. In general, the pattern should be symmetric about the center line of the door both vertically and horizontally. If this is too conservative for your tastes, then the same principles should be applied as in designing an oil painting.

The design should have balancing masses and an overall integrity, so that it does not look lopsided. The pattern should be laid out carefully on large graph paper and should be changed and changed until you are satisfied that it is exactly the shape that you want. Vertical and horizontal lines should be drawn through the exact center of the pattern. Similar vertical and horizontal lines should be drawn through the center lines of the wood panel which will form the door. The paper pattern should then be taped in place with carbon paper between the pattern and the wood. The design should then be transferred either using careful freehand drawing or using French curves or other appropriate guides.

The wooden board should then be clamped to the workbench or some other strong surface which will hold it rigidly during the carving. The pattern of the design should be cut into the wood using a chisel or sharp knife. The pattern should be cut in at least ⅛ inch deep. The interior portion of the pattern is then removed using a very sharp chisel. A ¼-inch wide flat chisel is a most useful tool for this wood removal.

The very center part of the pattern does not need to be depressed at all, as shown in the door detail of FIGURE 3. The depression should gradually deepen towards the borders of the pattern. After most of the wood is removed with a ¼-inch chisel, then wider ⅜ and ½-inch chisels may be used to even up the cut wood surfaces and smooth up and blend the profile. The final step is to sand the depressed areas to an even surface using coarse and then finer and finer grades of sandpaper.

FINISHING THE CABINET

All the electronic equipment and phonograph turntable should be removed before the finishing operations are performed. The first step is to hand-sand the wooden surfaces to a smooth finish.

An electric belt sander may be used, if the motion of the belt is kept parallel to the grain of the wood. Do not use any rotary sanding machine or fine circular marks will be cut into the wood which will stand out when the finish is applied.

The first finish is to seal the pores of the wood. A mixture of 50 per cent varnish and 50 per cent turpentine is excellent for this purpose. After the first coat of sealer has been placed on the wood, the grain will rise and have a fuzzy appearance. This fuzz should be sanded off using fine sandpaper, and a second and third coat of sealer applied.

For final finish, one of the very hard synthetic finishes was used. These synthetic finishes were in their infancy ten years ago, far better finishes are available today. A clear finish which will remain clear for many years is the best choice to bring out the beauty of the grain of the wood. The wood surface should be rubbed with steel wool before and after applying each coat of the final finish.

When all the finishing operations are completed, the doors should be fitted to the cabinet. Decorative hinges were installed on the sides of the door and an antiqued copper door pull was installed on each door close to the center line joint. Small detent buttons were recessed in the bottom of the doors with striker plates set into the top of the front facing board. These spring detent latches hold the doors in a closed position.

The final step in the assembly is to install the electronic components in the right-hand side of the cabinet and to install the phonograph turntable on the mahogany box. With these components in place and wired up, the backboard made of 3/16-or ¼-inch plywood should be installed on the back surface of the cabinet. It is nice to have a backboard which is mahogany one side, but if plain plywood is used this fact may be disguised by coating the plywood both sides with a mahogany-colored stain. The final step is to give the cabinet several coats of good furniture wax, and this should be delayed for several weeks until all of the solvents have evaporated from the finish.

The equipment may all be turned on and a stack of records placed in the phonograph, but no sound will emerge until you build the speaker cabinet described in the next chapter. The high-fidelity cabinet has the solid construction and intrinsic beauty that comes from well constructed furniture. It wears well, and the minor nicks and scratches of constant use do not disturb the warmth and good appearance of the cabinet.

6

High-Fidelity Speaker Cabinets

High-fidelity speaker cabinets come in many sizes and shapes, but most are very modern in their design. This speaker cabinet was designed to fit into an early American mode of decoration and still provide high-fidelity sound. The particular cabinet shown in these photographs is what is known as a "klipsch" cabinet, but I recommend that you construct what is known as a "bass reflex" type of cabinet for two reasons. The first is that the klipsch cabinet is a very complicated cabinet to construct. The second is that it must be placed in the corner of a room for best sound effect. Modern houses seldom have a corner which may be used for a speaker cabinet permanently, since the furniture arrangements keep changing.

A loudspeaker consists of a large disk of cardboard which is vibrated by an electric solenoid. As the cardboard disk vibrates, it generates sound on both sides of the disk. The sound at the front of the disk comes directly out the front of the speaker cabinet and is projected into the room. The sound generated on the back side of the speaker causes problems. If it is allowed to just echo around inside an ordinary wooden box, it will cause very bad echoes. The klipsch cabinet solves this problem by taking the sound from the back of the speaker and channeling it through a series of carefully designed passages so that it will properly reinforce the sound coming from the front of the speaker. The problem with the klipsch cabinet is its complicated construction.

The tremendous improvements in high-fidelity components during the past ten years make it unnecessary to use a complex cabinet design to achieve a really good high-fidelity sound. A bass reflex cabinet is much simpler to construct, and provides excellent performance with modern speakers. The bass reflex cabinet has an almost identical appearance to a klipsch cabinet from the front. The appearance of the cabinet is shown in FIGURE 1. The only difference is that the back of the klipsch cabinet is beveled off so that the top has a six-sided shape compared to a rectangular shape for the bass reflex cabinet.

The speaker cabinet is relatively economical to fabricate. Only the top and the sides need to be made from solid mahogany. It is very important that the cabinet be built of heavy materials with good bracing. If the back panel were of ¼-inch plywood, for example, it would vibrate with the loudspeaker and cause very bad echoes. Plywood ½ inch thick or thicker will provide a strong rigid structure which will not vibrate unless the speaker is driven very hard. The front panel on this hi-fi cabinet is actually made up of six different pieces of mahogany. Because the sections at the top and bottom are relatively thin and have the grain running crosswise, they were reinforced on the back with pieces of ¼-inch plywood.

The construction details are shown in FIGURE 2. The first step in construction is to purchase your high-fidelity speaker. This particular cabinet has been used with two different 12-inch "coaxial" speakers. All high-fidelity speakers consist of at least two units and sometimes three. A small speaker is used for the high frequency musical sound such as those coming from a violin. This is referred to as a "tweeter." A large-diameter speaker is used to provide the low-frequency sound such as that coming from bass drums or low piano notes. This is known as a "woofer." On some very high-quality speakers, a middle-range speaker is also provided to cover the middle-frequency span.

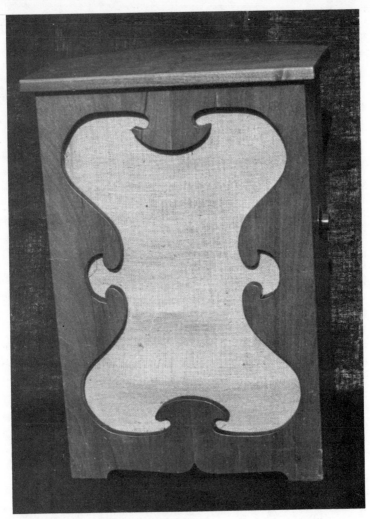

Figure 1

In a coaxial speaker the woofer and tweeter are built together as one unit with the high frequency speaker, the tweeter, on the center line of the instrument and the large diameter low frequency speaker mounted around it. Other speakers are sold

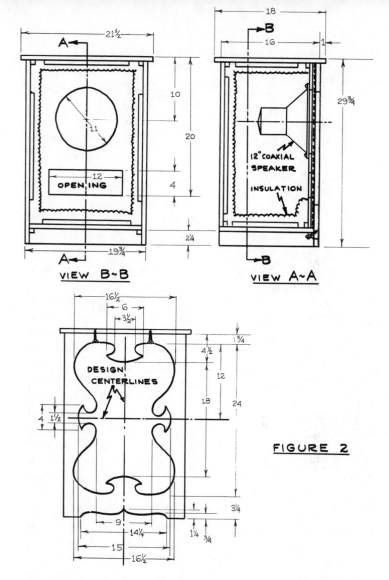

VIEW B~B

VIEW A~A

FIGURE 2

with separate elements, and these must be separately mounted in the speaker cabinet. This cabinet is large enough to handle almost any type of 12-inch speaker. A 15-inch speaker can be squeezed in, but there is only a marginal amount of space to handle the vibrations coming off this large speaker. When you purchase the speaker, be sure to get a template for mounting the components properly. If the woofer and tweeter are separate, see if there are instructions for mounting them some distance from each other. It is generally best to mount the large woofer on the center line, with the tweeter mounted diagonally to one side.

In a bass reflex cabinet the echoes from the rear of the speaker are absorbed by a heavy layer of 4-inch-thick fiberglass insulation as shown in *Views A-A* and *B-B* of FIGURE 2. The pure sound (without echoes) escapes from a 4 x 12-inch rectangular opening below the speaker.

The top of the cabinet is 21 inches long by 18 inches wide. This is made up from two pieces of mahogany glued together with $\frac{1}{4}$-inch dowels for alignment. The sides of the cabinet are 29 inches long by $15\frac{1}{4}$ inches wide. These must also be made up of two pieces glued together unless you are fortunate enough to find a board this wide. The piece of $\frac{1}{2}$-inch plywood should be cut $15\frac{1}{4}$ inches wide by 18 inches long. This forms the bottom shelf of the speaker cabinet. The corner joint construction is that shown in FIGURE 6 of Chapter 2. The top, two sides, and the bottom shelf should be assembled first. Two $\frac{3}{4}$-inch by $\frac{3}{4}$-inch strips of wood should be installed $\frac{1}{2}$ inch in from the back of the cabinet as shown in the side view of FIGURE 2. The back panel, which is 18 inches by 27 inches, should be cut from heavy plywood and should be checked very carefully to make sure that it is square. When the top, the sides, and the bottom have been assembled, but before the glue is dry, the rear panel should be installed and held in place with four or five screws as a means of providing exact alignment to keep the top and sides square with each other.

It is very important that the back panel not be glued in place, but merely held in place with screws. When these parts are thoroughly dried, $\frac{3}{4}$-inch by $\frac{3}{4}$-inch strips should be installed around the front face of the sides, top, and bottom to provide a fastening surface for the front board which holds the speakers. These strips should be installed about ½ inch back from the front surface, so that the speaker panel will fit flush with the sides. The speakers can then be mounted on the front board and the assembly installed in the speaker cabinet, and held in place with six to twelve screws.

The next step is to remove the rear panel. A heavy layer of fiberglass insulation 3 to 4 inches thick should be installed on the inside of the entire enclosure. A small cut can be made in the rear plywood board to allow the speaker wires to be led out the back of the cabinet.

Insulation should be placed on the inner surface of the rear board and it in turn may also be fastened in place. Balancing controls which balance the proportion of sound coming from the high frequency and low frequency speakers may most conveniently be located on the right-hand side of the speaker cabinet or on the back. These must be wired up before the rear panel is installed.

FRONT OF THE SPEAKER CABINET

The design of the front of the speaker cabinet is dimensioned on the right-hand side of FIGURE 2. The design follows that on the doors of the high-fidelity cabinet, but differs in proportions. The front assembly was actually made from six pieces of mahogany held together with dowels and glue.

The finished assembly is held to the speaker enclosure with two screws running up vertically as shown in the right-hand view of FIGURE 2, and several diagonal screws into the bottom of the assembly as shown in *View A-A* of FIGURE 2. The design of the front should be laid out on a large sheet of paper. The proportions may be changed to suit your preferences, or other designs substituted.

FINISHING THE CABINET

The same procedures and finish should be applied as on

the high-fidelity cabinet described in Chapter 5, so that the two pieces of furniture will match in warmth and texture.

FINAL ASSEMBLY

After the cabinet is finished and rubbed down, the wiring on the speaker and controls should be checked. A yard of light colored fine burlap should be purchased, and this should be trimmed to size and tacked in place over the front mounting board. If there are young children in the house, it is a good idea to tack some plastic screening over the speaker opening before installing the burlap. Sometimes this will save a valuable speaker from a puncture wound from a pencil or other childish probe.

After the burlap is smoothed in place the cutout mahogany assembly may be installed on the cabinet. Two screws hold the upper surface to the top of the cabinet, and three or four screws should be driven into the lower part of the mahogany as shown in *View A-A* of FIGURE 2.

Now you can wire up the speaker cabinet to the hi-fi, put on a stack of records and sit back and relax as glorious sound pours forth. Whether everyone agrees with the beauty of the sound depends on your choice of records. The high-fidelity assembly described in Chapters 5 and 6 have been well used for ten years. The turntable is constantly shifted from 45 rpm to 33 rpm and back as the choice moves from ballads to rock to classical and back again. All of the electronic equipment has been replaced with improved stereo models, and the changes were easily accomplished. The high-fidelity cabinet and speaker cabinet have provided years of durable service, and have retained a warm and fine appearance.

7

Glass-Topped Coffee Table

This coffee table is a small project which will provide many rewards. The table may be used to hold magazines, or it may be converted to display some special plants or flowers. It is designed with a large glass top 18 inches by 36 inches by ¼ inch thick. This glass is sturdy enough to take all normal adult abuse, and large enough to provide useful area for coffee, tea, or cocktails.

The glass-topped coffee table is shown in FIGURE 1 with the

Figure 1

lower shelf filled with magazines. The material on the lower shelf is attractively displayed, and it may also be used as the focal point for a display of small ceramics or statues instead of magazines.

A wooden cover board may be removed from the lower shelf revealing a long shallow cavity with a galvanized sheet metal tray neatly installed. The coffee table with the top board and metal tray removed is shown in FIGURE 2. The galvanized iron

Figure 2

tray is 8 inches wide by 2 inches deep, and 3 feet long. This pan should have soldered corner joints to be waterproof. It may be filled with pebbles and potted plants, or the plants may be placed directly in the tray.

The appearance of the table filled with plants is shown in FIGURE 3. For the nature lover this provides an excellent way to bring the freshness of growing plants right into the living room—even in the middle of a big city.

This table was constructed of mahogany, which is easy to

Figure 3

work and has an excellent appearance after finishing. The open grain of mahogany requires many finish coats for a really smooth surface. The quantity of wood is quite small, so that a wide variety of woods may be choosen without too much expense.

The dimensions of the coffee table are shown in FIGURE 4. The table is made up of many pairs of parts, which makes construction easier.

The top frame holding the glass should be constructed first. Cut the 13/16-inch-thick plank into strips 1¼ inches wide, with two strips 38 inches long, and two strips 19½ inches long. Notch the strips ¼ inch deep by ½ inch wide in order to take the glass and hold it securely. The shape of the wood in the top frame is shown in the *View A-A* of FIGURE 4. Glue the corners of the top frame together with blind wooden dowels running diagonally across the corner.

If you feel this is too difficult, then fasten the corners together with a long screw slightly countersunk below the sur-

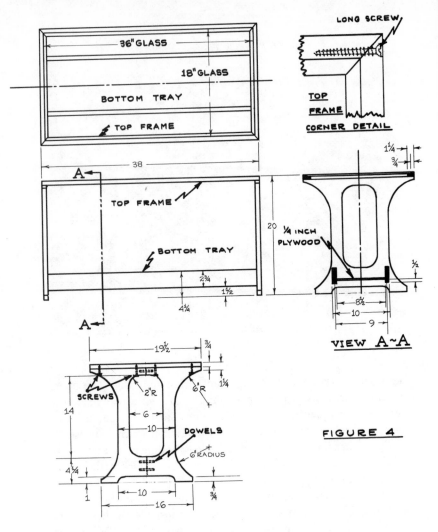

FIGURE 4

face as shown in the top frame corner detail of FIGURE 4. The top of the screw can be covered up with plastic wood to match the color of the wood used for the coffee table.

When you have set the top frame to dry, measure the diagonal length from one corner to the other. Compare this with the dimension across the other diagonal measurement. If these two diagonal measurements are not the same, then the entire frame is out of square. Check the length of each of the four sides, and then force the frame until the diagonals are equal. It is important that it be squared up before the glue dries or you will have a lopsided frame when you are finished. To hold the frame square it can be clamped to a sheet of plywood with C clamps.

The next parts to construct are the ends, which are each made up of two pieces of mahogany. The design of the ends should be laid out very carefully on a large sheet of paper. The proportions may be changed to suit your taste, and a number of decorative patterns may be substituted for the design shown. Transfer the shape to the boards using carbon paper. Extra wood should be left on the top and bottom surfaces to give good clamping surfaces for the gluing. Glue the end supports together with blind wooden dowels across the center line as shown in the left-hand side of FIGURE 4. After the glue has dried, saw off the clamping surfaces, file and sand the end supports to final shape.

Next construct the lower sides. These are pieces of wood 36½ inches long, 2¾ inches wide. Cut a ¼-inch-wide groove in these lower sides the full length. Cut a small sheet of plywood 9 inches wide by 36 inches long to form a floor for the bottom tray. The bottom floor is inset into the lower side as shown in *Section A-A* of FIGURE 4. This plywood does not have to be glued into place, since it is held captive by the sides.

ASSEMBLY OF THE COFFEE TABLE

The first step in assembling the coffee table is to fasten the lower sides to the ends. This may be done by marking their location very carefully on the ends, then drilling holes in the ends and in the lower rail to take blind dowels. The holes must be carefully located so that all of the parts line up after assembly. The ¼-inch plywood should be assembled to the lower sides. The ends are then smeared with glue, and dowels driven into the lower sides. When these are assembled in proper position on the ends, the blind dowels will slide into the holes which have been drilled in the ends.

The top frame is held on to the ends with glue and with four screws on each end. The location of these screws are shown on the end view of the coffee table on the left side of FIGURE 4. The holes in the ends should be drilled ahead of time and the heads of the screws countersunk into the wood.

The next step in assembly is to put a heavy layer of glue on the top surface of the ends and screw the top frame in place. The entire coffee table should be set on a level surface and checked to see that everything is flat and level. While on the level surface, clamps should be placed in line with the lower sides and end pressure placed on the end support to provide a good glued joint. The top frame will be held to the end supports by the screws which have been driven and this will set up into a good glued surface.

GALVANIZED TRAY

A small sketch of the galvanized tray is shown in FIGURE 5. The tray is 8¼ inches wide by 36 inches long and 2 inches deep. The tray used in this coffee table fits very closely. If you are trying to make the tray yourself, it is suggested that the width be cut to 8 inches and the length to 35¾ inches. The upper edges of this tray were rolled over to form a smooth upper surface and the corners were soldered. The result was a very sturdy and watertight tray.

The final element in the design was a top board of 10 inches wide by 36 inches long. This is shown on the right side of FIGURE 5. The board has been machined down at the edges so that it fits inside the galvanized tray. In this way the coffee table may be used either for holding magazines and books on the lower shelf with the top board in place, or it may be used as a planter, or for flower arrangements with the galvanized tray in place.

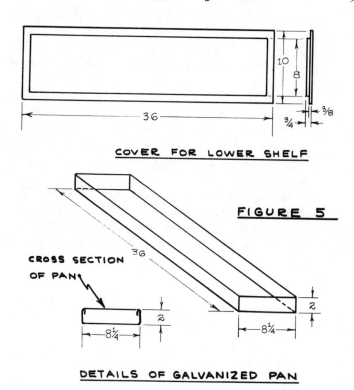

COVER FOR LOWER SHELF

FIGURE 5

CROSS SECTION OF PAN

DETAILS OF GALVANIZED PAN

GLASS TOP FOR THE TABLE

The coffee table is designed to take a sheet of plate glass ¼ inch thick, 18 inches wide, and 36 inches long. Tell the shop what the glass is to be used for and request that the edges be ground to a smooth surface. In most cases you will find that the glass has been cut exactly square and that the top frame of your coffee table is not exactly square. If you have been careful in gluing the top frame, the glass will set into the recess with minor chiseling at critical points in the frame.

This coffee table was finished with many coats of varnish. It should first be sanded to a smooth surface with a belt sander, or by hand sanding. The first coat of varnish should be diluted 50 per cent with turpentine. After the first coat, the grain will rise and the sanding should be repeated. Two more coats are applied with thinned varnish, and sanded after each coat. Two final coats of full strength varnish should be applied. The end supports and top frame are rubbed down with steel wool in between each of these coats.

The final result is an attractive coffee table that provides a great deal of flexibility for modern living. This flexibility allows changing displays in the coffee table with changing seasons, or the placement of special displays for parties or other occasions.

8

Gun Cabinet
or Display Cabinet

This chapter describes the construction of a large standing cabinet which provides an ideal place for the locked storage of firearms. The cabinet is constructed with a pegboard back so that a wide variety of objects may be displayed on the back wall. By minor modifications in the design shelves may be installed on the back wall, creating a glass-fronted bookcase, or a cabinet for the display of valuable collections. A hidden light is installed just underneath the top of the cabinet which provides illumination across the entire display area.

The cabinet is shown in FIGURE 1 with a full complement of firearms. The guns range from a Pennsylvania muzzle-loading target rifle dating from about 1830 through a series of Civil War breech-loading rifles up to a modern .22 caliber bolt action rifle with a large 24-power telescopic sight, and the latest model slide-action shotgun. The cabinet provides a secure and attractive storage for the fourteen guns on display.

The gun cabinet has been moved outdoors and the doors opened to show more of the internal details in FIGURE 2. The pegboard back to the cabinet is clearly visible in this illustration. Five antique swords and an ancient cap and ball pistol have been wired to the pegboard to form a background for the gun display. Any objects may easily be fastened to the

Figure 1

Figure 2

backboard either using copper wire or standard hooked fasteners designed for pegboard. The glass fronted doors are partially open in FIGURE 2 and the keys which are used to lock the cabinet may be seen on the right-hand door. At the center of the cabinet fastened to the underside of the top is a board about 10 inches long and 3 inches wide. This board serves as a stop for the two doors in the closed position. Installed directly behind it are the light fixtures which provide illumination for the entire cabinet.

It is easy to visualize a series of five or six shelves in the cabinet instead of the one upper gun rack. The shelves may be made of wood and positioned by metal tracks such as those used in the bookcase described in Chapter 3. For really fancy construction, glass shelves can be installed with the mounting brackets attached to the rear pegboard.

The construction details of the cabinet are shown in FIGURE 3. The general shape of the cabinet is shown in the front and side views. A cross section of the cabinet is shown in the right-hand side in *View C-C*. The position of the upper and lower gun racks and the light for illumination is clearly shown in this illustration.

The positioning of the gun racks is shown in *View A-A* which is the horizontal section through the cabinet. The upper gun rack detail is also shown in the upper right-hand corner of the illustration. The upper gun rack is installed 32 inches above the base of the cabinet, while the buttstocks of the rifles are positioned by a series of shallow wooden boxes constructed on the floor of the cabinet.

The top of the gun cabinet is made from a plank of mahogany four feet long by 14 inches wide. This is trimmed to a finished length of 47 inches long and a finished width of 13½ inches. The edges were rounded with molding cutters giving the same shape as the bookcase described in Chapter 3. This is really an added touch and it is perfectly acceptable to leave the edges square. The sides of the cabinet are made from two pieces of mahogany 53 inches long by 11 inches wide. The bottom is made from two pieces, one 1½ inches wide by 42½ inches long, and the other 9½ inches by 42½ inches long.

The lower panel is made from a piece of mahogany 5 inches wide by 44 inches long. An early American design was cut into this panel to a height of 2 inches and a width of 34 inches. The lower rack is installed at an angle in the bottom of the cabinet as shown in *View C-C* of FIGURE 3. This type of in-

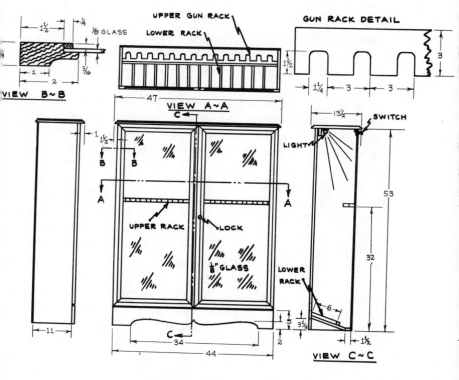

FIGURE 3

stallation accomplishes two things. First, it brings the front of the rack above the cutout portion of the lower panel so that it is invisible. The second thing is that the guns are held by the toe of the stock in a very firm position. If the lower rack were installed perfectly flat, the stocks would be held by the heel and the guns would tend to flop around into awkward positions.

The first step in assembly is to install ¾ x ¾-inch filler blocks on the two side boards in the proper position to hold the top and the lower rack. The filler blocks have been eliminated from FIGURE 3, to simplify the drawing, but they are installed at the upper edge of the sides, and also in an angled position at the bottom to accept the lower rack. The construction is that shown in FIGURE 6 of Chapter 2, with glue smeared on the filler blocks, and screws driven in to the two pieces of wood to be assembled.

The first step in assembly is to fasten the top, the two sides, and the bottom together. In order to get the construction exactly square, it is quite useful to fasten the lower panel in place at the same time. Diagonal measurements should be taken across the face of the cabinet to be sure that it is exactly square. One way of holding it square while the glue is drying it to cut the pegboard back assembly which is 53 inches high by 43½ inches wide and install this to the sides with screws.

While the main assembly is drying, you can proceed with the upper rack. Design of the upper rack should be modified depending on the type of guns you wish to display. If you have double-barrel shotguns, the width of the slot should be increased to about 2 inches, but the center-to-center spacing does not need to be increased. The 3-inch spacing allows the display of fourteen guns. Some bolt action rifles give problems with the spacing and must be stored with the bolt open. Some rifles such as lever action models allow spacing as close as 2½ inches, but the three inch spacing provides broad flexibility for a changing display of different types of firearms.

The upper rack on this cabinet was installed into slots

machined in the side walls. This is an excellent construction, but really not necessary. The construction shown in FIGURE 6 of Chapter 2 may be used or the upper rack may merely be fastened to the rear pegboard with screws.

The lower rack is constructed of a number of pieces of ¾ x ¾-inch mahogany. Thirteen pieces 6 inches long are required and one piece 42½ inches long. The easy way to build the lower rack is to finish sand each of the pieces, then smear one surface with glue. Position the strip properly on the bottom of the cabinet and nail it in place with two small finishing nails. The finishing nails are nearly invisible after all the work is done, and it is a very easy method of construction.

DOORS

The doors are constructed out of strips of wood 2 inches wide by ¾ inch thick. In constructing this cabinet, I experimented with various shapes and finally evolved a cross section shown in *View B-B* of FIGURE 3. A notch 5/16 inch deep by ½ inch wide was cut on the inside of the frame to accept the glass. One-eighth-inch-thick glass was installed and small 3/16-inch by ¼-inch wood strips were used to hold the glass in place. These wood battens were fastened to the main part of the frame with small finishing nails.

In order to give the doors additional character, a scalloped cut one inch wide by 3/16 inch deep was made on the outer surface. This gives the doors somewhat the appearance of a picture frame and cast shadows which make the cabinet more interesting. Four strips of wood should be cut each slightly over 4 feet long and four other strips each slightly over 22 inches long. The corners of the doors should be cut at a 45° angle and the corner joints should be constructed as shown in the "Top Frame Corner Detail" shown in FIGURE 4 of Chapter 7.

The diagonal cut should be smeared with glue, drilled and

the long screw driven in to draw the joint up properly. The doors should each be 22 inches wide and should have a finished height of slightly under 48 inches. It is impossible to get the doors to exactly the right dimensions and exactly square, but it is important to make them as close as possible. The way to check that the doors are rectangular is to measure the dimension across the diagonals. It is usually a good idea to clamp the doors to a flat surface while the glue is drying and final adjustments can be made to square up the doors using clamps.

The doors should be installed on the cabinet using antiqued copper hinges or another good quality decorative type of hinge. Fitting the doors will take planing and sanding at critical spots to get the doors to hang just right. It is well to defer purchasing the glass until after the cabinet is completely sanded and finished since the thin sheets are fragile until supported by the door frame. When it is time, measure the exact inside dimensions of the recess and subtract about ⅛ inch from the length and width. If you are very brave, you can reduce the dimension by only 1/16 inch and chisel the recess to allow the glass to slide into place. The glass and door will rarely match exactly and some fitting is to be expected.

INSTALLATION OF HARDWARE AND LIGHTS

After the doors are installed, you will notice that there is nothing to prevent the doors from swinging too far inward. This problem is solved by installing a board 2 inches wide by about 14 inches long in the center of the cabinet which acts as a stop. This board is shown fastened to the top of the cabinet in *View C-C* of FIGURE 3. Immediately behind this board the author installed an aluminum reflector made of some scrap aluminum sheeting and two electric sockets facing outwards from the center of the cabinet. A long narrow 25-watt bulb was installed in each socket which provides good illumination across the interior of the gun cabinet. The wires from the sockets were stapled to the inside of the top of the gun cabinet and run to the rear where a switch was installed in the top surface of the pegboard.

The lights may be operated by reaching over the top of the gun cabinet and flicking the exposed switch. The switch installation is only visible from the front of the cabinet if you look upward into the cabinet from the front. It proves to be a very satisfactory installation providing excellent illumination for the objects on display.

A small brass stop was installed at the center of the lower panel on the back surface to prevent the bottom of the doors from swinging in too far. A sliding door stop was installed on the left-hand door. When this stop is slid downward, it locks the bottom of the door securely to the lower panel of the gun cabinet. A small lock and striker plate were installed in the right-hand door. This lock has a tongue which projects behind the left hand door thus locking the cabinet from casual entry. The sequence to completely open the cabinet is to insert the key in the lock, rotate the lock, and open the right-hand door. You can then reach in behind the left-hand door and raise the bolt which locks the left-hand door shut swinging that door open as well. It is obvious that if anyone is seriously intent on opening the cabinet, they can always accomplish this by smashing the glass, but the lock does prevent children or anyone else from casually handling the guns or other objects on display.

FINISHING THE GUN CABINET

Finishing this gun cabinet is similar to the procedure used on the other furniture described in this book. It is well to do finished sanding on the upper gun rack, the doors, and the strips used up to make the lower gun rack before they are installed in the cabinet. Some additional sanding must be done after final assembly to smooth up slight imperfections.

Figure 4

The first coats of finish should seal the pores of the wood. An open-grained wood such as mahogany requires about three coats of sealer, while a closer grained wood such as maple or cherry requires fewer coats. The first coat should be a thin material such as shellac or a mixture of 50 per cent varnish and 50 per cent turpentine. The first coat may be placed on with a relatively dry brush and with care being used not to get drip marks on the wood.

After this coat is dry, the grain will be raised and the fuzz should be removed with fine sandpaper. Two more sealer coats with sanding in between will provide an excellent basis for the final finishing operations. A non-yellowing varnish or one of the new synthetic materials may be used to bring out the true beauty of the wood and provide a hard, long lasting finish. Adequate time should be allowed for the finish to completely dry in between coats. It is well to rub down with steel wool to develop a smooth-textured finish.

CONCLUSIONS

The design of the cabinet may be modified to fit your own particular needs. The basic design is suitable for the display of a wide variety of objects from firearms to cut glass and china to minerals or insect collections. The design may be altered by installation of a series of small shelves, a few large shelves or even glass shelves to adopt a design to your own particular needs and interests. The cabinet design is relatively simple to construct and has given excellent service over the past seven years.

9

The Early American Hutch

The colonists came to America in small sailing vessels which were incredibly crowded by modern standards. Passengers spent an average of three months of pitching and rolling in these vessels, which must be visited to be believed. On many ships there wasn't even enough room to stand upright below decks. Passengers slept and ate in communal rooms which were filled with hammocks at night, and cleared as a common room during the day. The deck was the only place where really fresh air was available. An extremely small percentage of colonists had anything approaching a simple cramped cabin.

Space throughout these tiny ships was at a premium, so that cargo was limited to essential supplies for the voyage plus firearms, ammunition, tools, materials for trading with the Indians, and a few scanty household goods. Furniture is both bulky and fragile, and with few exceptions it was left behind in England or Europe by the colonists.

The first order of business in the New World was to arrange for food, shelter, and a military security system. Once these had been solved, furniture and housewares became the next order of business. Three-legged stools could be made from available wood with very little labor. Beds were made with a wooden frame, and cross-laced ropes served as a crude springing system for a thin mattress or plain blankets. Dishes, spoons, and forks were carved from wood, and the colonists' hunting knives were often used for table service as well.

All humans yearn for the "better things" of life, and the household furnishings were constantly improved and upgraded as quickly as time or money were available. The three-legged stool was replaced by a slat-back chair, which was originally made from 1-to 2-inch-diameter poles cut from the woods. After the wood was seasoned, two front legs were cut about 18 inches long, and two long pieces were cut about 3 to 4 feet long. The longer pieces served as the rear legs and the back of the chair. The four legs were held in position by horizontal "stretchers" which also formed the framework for the seat of the chair. The name "slat-back" comes from the curved thin slats which were split from a tree, and fitted between the two tall poles at the back of the chair. These horizontal slats provided something to lean against. Most chairs had either three or four slats, but some had as many as six horizontal slats, depending on the inclination of the furniture maker.

The slat-back style became very popular since it was handy, inexpensive and light. The woven rope or rush seat was comfortable even if the back of the chair was too straight for modern day standards. During the first two hundred years of the colonies over fifty different types of chairs were produced in America. Even the slat-back was upgraded to a style with which we are familiar today, with turned legs and stretchers, and curved slats of varying widths forming the back of the chair. Many were painted to provide more color in the colonial homes.

The early colonists brought their meager household goods in wooden crates, and these were used as storage chests and seats in the log cabins of the early era. When more money was available the colonists replaced their wooden bowls and cups with pewter dishes and mugs. The wooden spoons and forks were replaced with pewter or silver utensils.

The metal housewares represented a great step forward in furnishings and in status and prestige of the owners. Who would want to bury such hard-earned finery in a chest when it was not in use? The desire to display pewter, silver, and glass properly led to the development of the "hutch." This was a piece of furniture which combined the storage capability of the early chests in a lower section, and added an upper section with open display shelves. Hutches were constructed in many sizes and shapes to fit the needs of the times. The one described in this chapter is relatively tall and narrow, with a width of only a little over 2 feet, and a height of about 6 feet.

The finished hutch is shown in FIGURE 1, and the design is shown in FIGURE 2. This design includes three storage shelves in the lowest section, which are covered by a carved door. Above the storage area is a single drawer, which provides a fine storage place for gloves and scarves, if the hutch is kept in an entrance hallway.

The upper section is set back from the lower storage area, as shown in the side view of FIGURE 2. The set-back provides a broad shelf, which is a handy place to put things such as hats or keys as you go in or out of your home. Sometimes this space proves to be too handy, and becomes piled high with the small items of modern living, but these can be swept off into the drawer, if they remain too long. The area in the rear of the set-back is a display space for small objects which are somewhat protected by the side panels.

The main display area is provided by the three upper shelves. These have a scalloped design shown in the "Shelf Detail" of FIGURE 3. A shallow groove at the rear of the shelf holds the edge of dishes which are displayed vertically. An ornate copper and silver dish is shown on an upper shelf of the hutch in FIGURE 1.

This hutch was constructed entirely with hand tools and with no workbench available. The parts were cut by hand using the techniques shown in the "Lower Panel Detail" in FIGURE 12 of Chapter 2. Cutting the side panels, top facing board and shelves by hand methods is time consuming, but it can be done, and is the way that all of the original hutch designs were created.

The construction details of the hutch are shown in FIGURE 2

Figure 1

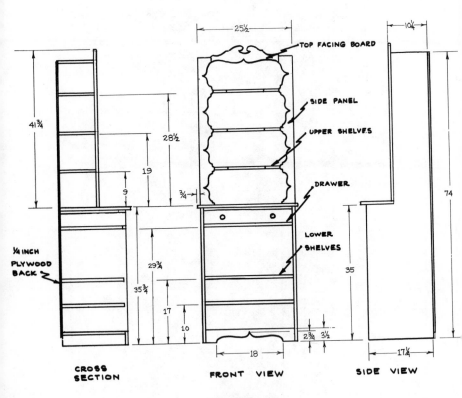

FIGURE 2

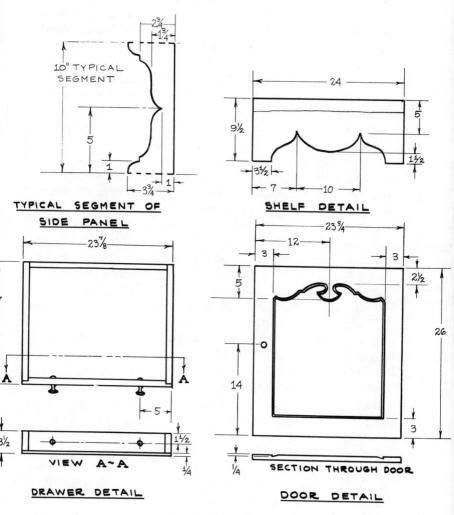

TYPICAL SEGMENT OF
SIDE PANEL

SHELF DETAIL

DRAWER DETAIL

VIEW A~A

DOOR DETAIL

SECTION THROUGH DOOR

FIGURE 3

and FIGURE 3. It was constructed of a low cost material known as "Number Two Shelving." This is pine wood which is blemished by knots. The wood must be very carefully selected at the lumberyard so that you do not get planks with loose knots which will fall out during construction. The planks must also be carefully examined to be sure they are not twisted, as twisted wood makes good construction almost impossible. The knotty pattern of the shelving makes a very interesting design in the finished furniture.

The first step in construction is to lay out the design of the shelves, top facing board and side panels on paper in full size. The design of the side panels is such that the pattern is repeated four times on each tide. It is only necessary to lay out the design of one section and then transfer it to the board using carbon paper at four successive locations. The top facing board is symmetric about the center line of the hutch and only one half must be laid out. It is a good idea to take a large sheet of paper and fold it over double. The design may be laid out on one side of the sheet of paper and then transferred to the other side with carbon paper. When the sheet is opened up you can get the view of the entire design.

The top facing board and side panels can most easily be cut out on a jigsaw or bandsaw. If neither is available, the technique shown in FIGURE 12 of Chapter 2 should be used. A series of saw cuts are made, and the material in between the cuts is removed with a wood chisel, and then the curved shape is smoothed up with rasps and files. The three upper shelves are identical in dimensions and are shown in the "Shelf Detail" of FIGURE 3. They have a scalloped design which gives rounded contours to the display area and adds interest to the objects on the shelves. Along the back of the shelf a shallow groove has been cut to hold the bottom of dishes which are displayed vertically.

The sides of the cabinet are made of two boards edge glued together. One board is 74 inches long, and nominal 10 inches wide. The other board is 35 inches long and a nominal 8 inches wide. These boards should be edge glued together with dowels using the technique shown in FIGURE 11 of Chapter 2.

In addition to the upper shelves, a top board, large center shelf (located at the set-back of the cabinet) and the lower shelves should be cut to size and sanded smooth.

The entire cabinet is assembled by the simplest possible techniques. The ends of the lower shelves are smeared with glue and then held in place by small finishing nails driven in through the sides of the cabinet. The upper shelves are also held in with small finishing nails which are countersunk below the surface of the wood. After the construction is completed and the glue has dried, plastic wood is placed in the holes over the nails.

The back of the hutch is made from ¼-inch-thick plywood. The back may be temporarily fastened in place to hold the sides and shelves in alignment while the glue dries. The way to check if everything is square is to measure the diagonal distance from the right bottom of the hutch to the left top. This dimension should be exactly the same as the diagonal measurement from the lower left-hand corner of the cabinet to the upper right-hand corner.

The next step in assembly is to add the top facing board, the two side panels, and the lower panel. Each of these is held in place with glue, and small finishing nails driven in below the surface of the wood.

DOOR

The door at the front of the hutch is constructed of three pieces of shelving edge glued with dowels as shown in FIGURE 11 of Chapter 2. The details of the door are shown in the lower right side of FIGURE 3. The design on the front of the door repeats the design of the top facing board, and the same paper pattern may be used, with minor modifications to fit the door

Figure 4

width. The pattern was transferred to the door with carbon paper, and then cut into the wood surface with a sharp knife and chisel as shown in the "Section Through Door" in FIGURE 3.

DRAWER

The drawer for the hutch was constructed as shown in the "Drawer Detail" of FIGURE 3. It is a simple box built of ¾-inch-thick wood with a ¼-inch-thick plywood bottom. The sides and bottom should be rabbeted into the front so that they do not show when the drawer is closed. Antique brass door-pulls were installed on the drawer to permit easy opening.

FINISHING THE HUTCH

After the hutch is fully assembled and all the glued joints have dried, the wood should be sanded by hand, or with a vibrating or belt sander. Do not use a rotary sander, or cuts will be put into the wood across the grain, and these will show up clearly as dark scratches. The hutch was finished with a stain which contains a great deal of wax. The wood was lightly sanded after staining, and then many coats of wax were added to develop a tough, durable surface.

The hutch is a very flexible and useful piece of furniture. The design is deeply rooted in America's colonial heritage, and it provides an excellent display area for glass, china, copper, pewter, or ceramics. The construction is relatively simple, and the hutch provides a useful and interesting addition to your home.

Index